Grade
2

Summer Activities
for the Gifted Student

Written by **Kathy Furgang**

Illustrations by **Jannie Ho**

FlashKids

An imprint of Sterling Children's Books

Published by Sterling Publishing Co., Inc.
387 Park Avenue South, New York, NY 10016
Text and illustrations © 2010 by Flash Kids
Distributed in Canada by Sterling Publishing
c/o Canadian Manda Group, 165 Dufferin Street
Toronto, Ontario, Canada M6K 3H6
Distributed in the United Kingdom by GMC Distribution Services
Castle Place, 166 High Street, Lewes, East Sussex, England BN7 1XU
Distributed in Australia by Capricorn Link (Australia) Pty. Ltd.
P.O. Box 704, Windsor, NSW 2756, Australia

Cover image © P. Broze & A. Chederros/Getty Images
Cover design and production by Mada Design, Inc.

Sterling ISBN 978-1-4114-2762-4

Manufactured in Canada

Lot #:
2   4   6   8   10   9   7   5   3
02/12

For information about custom editions, special sales, premium and
corporate purchases, please contact Sterling Special Sales
Department at 800-805-5489 or specialsales@sterlingpublishing.com.

Learning doesn't have to stop when the school year ends. *Summer Activities for the Gifted Student* offers thought-provoking exercises designed to challenge advanced learners during the vacation months. It reviews familiar skills and introduces new ones, all the while providing your child with the intellectual stimulation gifted children crave.

This workbook provides activities that challenge your child's unique abilities in all subject areas—language arts, math, social studies, and science. All materials presented here are carefully calibrated to match the average reading level, analytical capability, and subject interest of a gifted second grader. Reading passages present new vocabulary, math problems encourage critical-thinking skills, and writing exercises promote creativity. Science and social studies activities introduce new concepts while testing logic and problem-solving skills.

A few activities in this book will require finding additional information using outside sources such as an encyclopedia, a dictionary, or the Internet. Helping your child complete these exercises provides an opportunity to teach valuable research skills. In fact, all of the activities in this book provide a chance to work with your child to offer advice, guidance, praise, and encouragement. Have a wonderful summer and, most of all, have fun learning with your child!

In the Jungle

What animal do you see here? Connect the dots by 4s to find out.

Word Start-Up

Look at each picture. Write the letters that blend to make the beginning sound of each word.

1. _fl_ ower

2. _ch_ icken

3. _pl_ anet

4. _ch_ erry

5. _sk_ ream

6. _fl_ ag

7. _sl_ ed

8. _ph_ one

5

Where in the World?

Complete each sentence below to show the many ways to describe where you live.

1. The number of the building or house I live in is _a house_.

2. The name of my street is _Captin pesivel_

3. The name of my town is _South Yarmuth_.

4. The name of my county is _Barnstable_.

5. The name of my state is _Massachusetts_

6. The name of my country is _USA_.

7. The name of my continent is _America_.

8. The name of my planet is _earth_.

Busy Seasons!

Match each season to the activities that are done in it.
There will be two activities for each season.

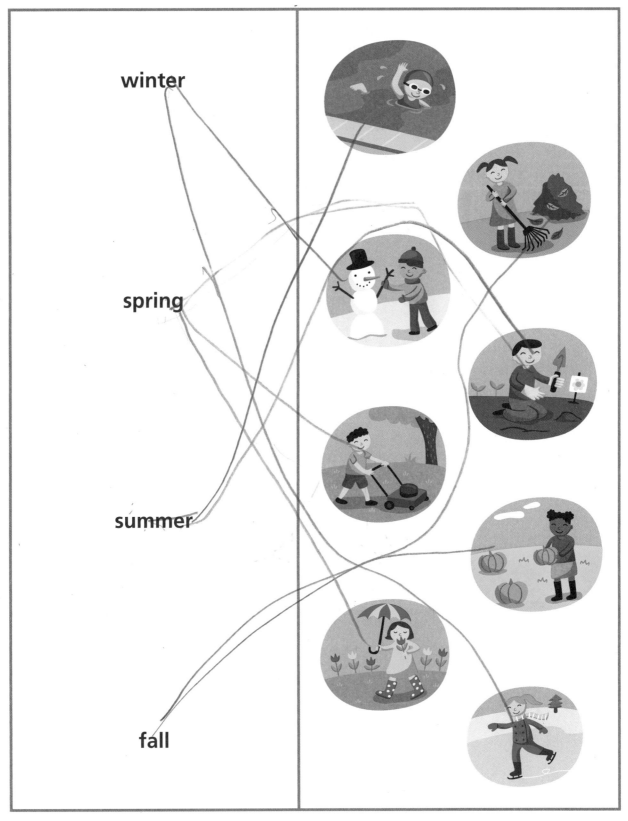

winter

spring

summer

fall

What a Treasure!

Connect the dots by 6s to find out what is on the beach.

A Blending Ending

Look at each picture. Write the letters that blend to make the ending sound of each word.

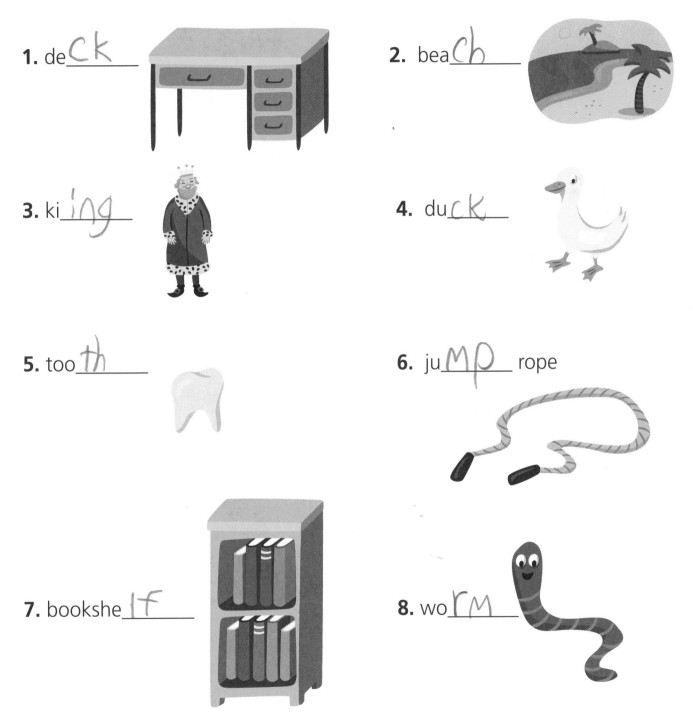

1. de<u>ck</u>

2. bea<u>ch</u>

3. ki<u>ing</u>

4. du<u>ck</u>

5. too<u>th</u>

6. ju<u>mp</u> rope

7. bookshe<u>lf</u>

8. wo<u>rm</u>

Sink or Float?

Circle the items next to the bathtub that you think will float. Then draw an item in the water that you think will float. Test your idea.

Buddies in a Row

Look at the patterns on the kids' T-shirts. Figure out the patterns and write the missing number or numbers in each pattern.

1. 12 14 16 18 20 22

2. 5 10 15 20 25 30

3. 50 60 70 80 90 100

4. 25 35 45 55 65 75

Which One Is More?

Write < or > to show which number is greater.

1. 255  349

2. 399  431

3. 572  527

4. 927  903

5. 354 > 640

6. 231 < 214

7. 393 > 461

8. 468 > 623

9. 540  499

10. 821  921

12

Whose Job Is It?

Read the description of each job. Write the name of the person who does each job.
Use the words in the word bank to help you.

> chef   construction worker   waiter   photographer
> mail carrier   doctor   firefighter   pilot
> musician   zookeeper

1. This person makes sick people feel better. _Doctor_

2. This person brings food to people in a restaurant. _Waiter_

3. This person feeds animals at a zoo. _Zookeeper_

4. This person flies airplanes. _Pilot_

5. This person cooks food for people in a restaurant. _Chef_

6. This person delivers packages and letters. _Mail carrier_

7. This person puts out fires. _Firefiters_

8. This person builds houses. _Construction worker_

9. This person plays a musical instrument. _Musician_

10. This person takes pictures. _photographer_

Short E Everywhere

Say the name of each object in the park.
Circle the objects that have a **short e** sound.

Ladybug Button

Summer was almost over. Ladybug Button flew up to a cozy home. She landed on the kitchen window sill. She squeezed under the screen as usual. She nibbled lazily for hours on the tiny scraps of food. Then she began to fly around the house. She landed behind the large rocking chair and looked around for food. She took off again and flew from room to room. Suddenly, she realized that she was lost! How would she ever find her way back to the kitchen window in this huge house? She began to panic. Outside she heard rain and wind hitting the house. This made her think. "What's wrong with staying in this nice house, anyway? It would make a fine home," she said. It would keep her safe and warm. Ladybug Button was glad she had found a good spot to stay for the winter.

Answer the questions about the story.

1. What is the main idea of the story?

_____

_____

2. What is the setting of the story?

_____

_____

3. What happens at the end of the story?

_____

_____

Where's the Reptile?

Circle the animal in each row that is a reptile.

Mixed-Up Traffic

Look at each group of cars. Color the car with the greatest number blue.
Color the car with the lowest number yellow.

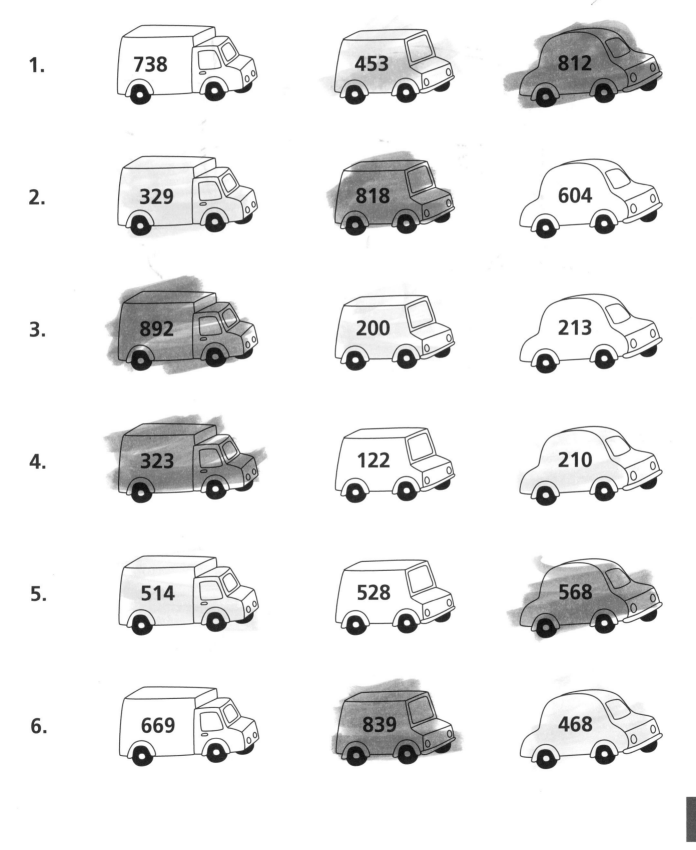

1. 738 453 812

2. 329 818 604

3. 892 200 213

4. 323 122 210

5. 514 528 568

6. 669 839 468

Mixed-Up Parade

The kids in the parade are out of order.
Rewrite their numbers in the correct order from least to greatest.

1. 221 700 160 800

160 221 700 800

2. 911 918 932 929

911 918 929 932

3. 421 713 306 272

_____ _____ _____ _____

4. 882 436 202 611

_____ _____ _____ _____

5. 370 902 102 709

_____ _____ _____ _____

6. 370 902 102 709

_____ _____ _____ _____

Which Does Not Belong?

Circle the word in each row that does not have the same vowel sound as the others.

1. pool   shoe   (rose)   tool   grew

2. tree   believe   green   leave   (apple)

3. corn   horn   born   (bone)   boar

4. caught   jar   (thought)   paw   jaw

5. late   great   (lamb)   plate   trait

6. (should)   high   cry   fly   sigh

Celebrate the Holidays!

Write the name of each holiday on the line.
Use the names of the holidays in the word bank.

**Thanksgiving   Halloween   New Year's Eve   4th of July
Earth Day   Memorial Day   Valentine's Day**

1. On this holiday we count down to the beginning of January 1.

_____

2. On this holiday people dress up in costumes.

Halloween

3. On this holiday we celebrate the birthday of the nation.

_____

4. On this holiday we celebrate the people we love.

Valentines day

5. On this holiday we celebrate the things for which we are thankful.

thanksgiving

6. On this holiday we celebrate ways we can protect our environment.

earth Day

Needs and Wants

Do you know your needs and wants? On the left of the chart make a list of things you need. On the right of the chart make a list of things you want.

Needs	Wants

Are there more things you need or more things you want? _____

Which Comes from Plants?

Circle the food in each row that is made from plants.

1.

2.

3.

4.

Look inside your refrigerator. Can you identify which foods come from plants and which don't? Make a list.

Foods from plants	Foods **not** from plants

Busy Becky

Read each sentence. Circle three action words in each sentence.

1. Becky made a bowl of cereal, ate it, and then raced to school.

2. After reading in class, Becky closed the book and wrote her report.

3. Mom cooked dinner, then Becky cleared the table and washed the dishes.

4. Should Becky look in the yard for the toys she lost, or search in her room?

5. Becky saw Max burying his bone after barking and digging in the yard for an hour.

6. Becky brushed her teeth, took a shower, and put on her pajamas.

Colors Everywhere

Look at the shapes and colors in each row. Draw to continue each pattern.

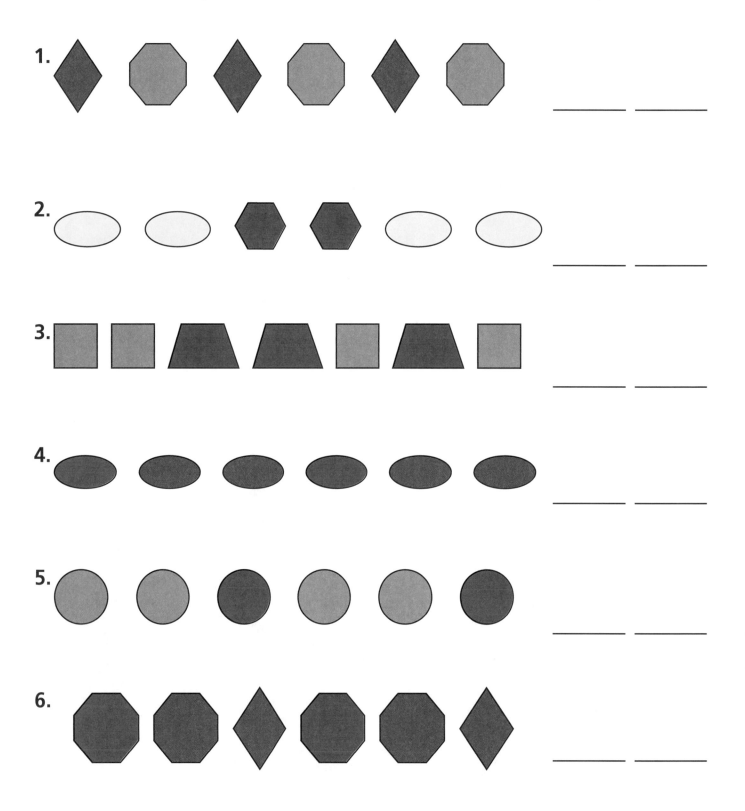

Captain Dave

Dave had been waiting to go on this family cruise for months. It was everything he had imagined it would be. He loved walking around the ship and seeing all the people who worked there. He imagined how fun it would be to work on a cruise ship when he grew up. But what job would he want to do on the ship?

The most important person on the cruise ship was the captain. Dave decided he was going to be a cruise ship captain someday. One night his parents met the captain. They introduced Dave to him. The captain brought Dave to the bridge of the ship. That's where everything was controlled. Dave was amazed. The captain told Dave that if he worked hard in school, he could be a ship captain, too, and that's just what Dave decided to do.

Write **true** or **false** after each sentence from the story.

1. Dave had waited for months to go on a cruise with his family.

_____

2. The ship was not as fun as Dave had expected. _____

3. Dave decided that he never wanted to go on a cruise ship again.

_____

4. Dave met the captain and saw the bridge of the ship. _____

5. The captain told Dave that he could one day be a ship captain, too.

_____

Know Your Own Information

Fill out the information about yourself below.

First and last name _____

Address _____

_____

Home phone number _____

Police phone number _____

Year you were born _____

Parents' names _____

Brothers' and sisters' names _____

_____

In case of an emergency, call _____ at
_____.

Symbols of Our Nation

Complete each sentence with the name of the American symbol.

1. The national bird of the United States is the _____.

2. The place where the U.S. president lives and works is called the
_____.

3. A statue that is a symbol of America's freedom is the _____.

4. We pledge our allegiance to the American _____.

5. What does the word "freedom" mean?

_____

_____

_____

_____

Using Your Senses

Write the name of the two senses that are most needed to experience each item below.

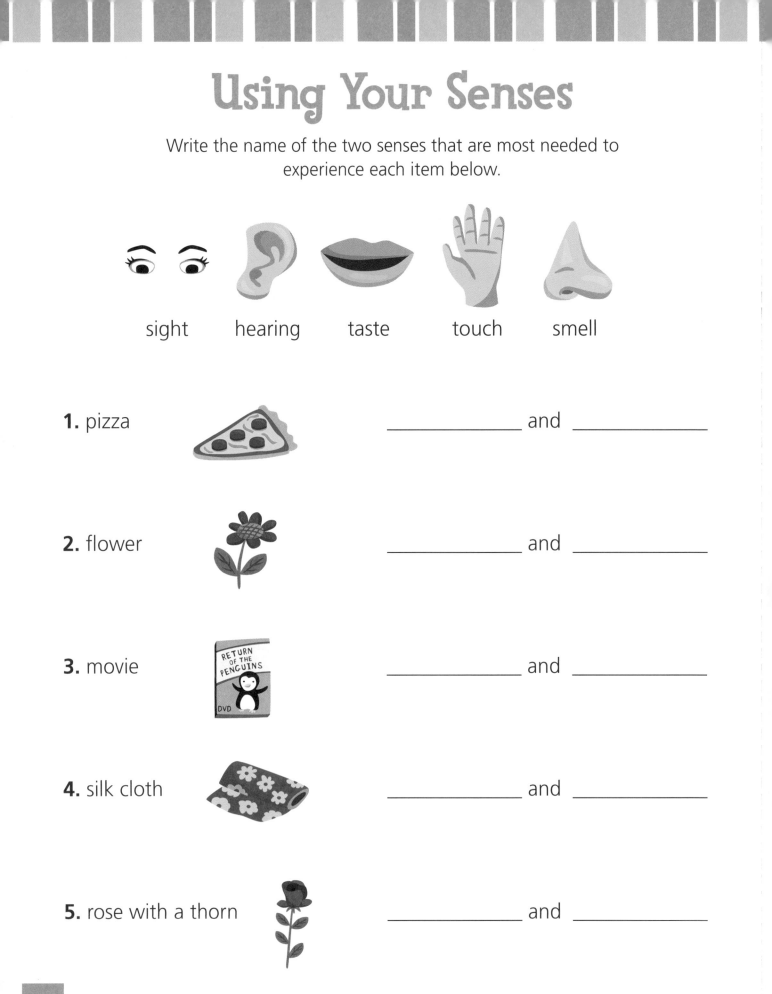

sight   hearing   taste   touch   smell

1. pizza   _____ and _____

2. flower   _____ and _____

3. movie   _____ and _____

4. silk cloth   _____ and _____

5. rose with a thorn   _____ and _____

Mix and Match

Find the shirt and hat with the same pattern. Draw a line to connect them.

Find the Lowest

Circle the card in each group with the lowest number.

1.

7,200   2,394   2,304

2.
1,992   1,009   1,293

3.

1,004   1,040   1,400

4.
8,203   2,300   3,200

5.

2,933   3,033   2,033

6.
993   1,999   1,009

A Born Explorer

Meghan knows that she can be whatever she wants to be when she grows up. One day she decided she would become a cowgirl. She would go out west and explore undiscovered land.

"That's a nice idea," said her mom. "But all the land in the United States has already been explored. There aren't too many cowboys or cowgirls left in the West." Meghan was sad at this news. "You could play a cowgirl in a show or circus," her mom added to make her feel better.

Meghan was determined to explore new places. "I know!" she said. "I'll explore space! I'm going to grow up and be an astronaut."

Answer the questions about the story. Circle the letter of the correct answer.

1. What do you think the word **determined** in paragraph 3 means?
   a. serious about something
   b. sad about something
   c. confused about something

2. Why do you think a circus might have a cowgirl in a show?
   a. to explore the audience
   b. to teach the audience
   c. to entertain the audience

3. How is a cowgirl like an astronaut?
   a. both explore space
   b. both explore new places
   c. both ride a horse

Plant Parts

Draw a line from each plant part name to the place where it is on the plant. Then draw another line to match each plant part to the job it does.

stem		holds up the plant
leaf	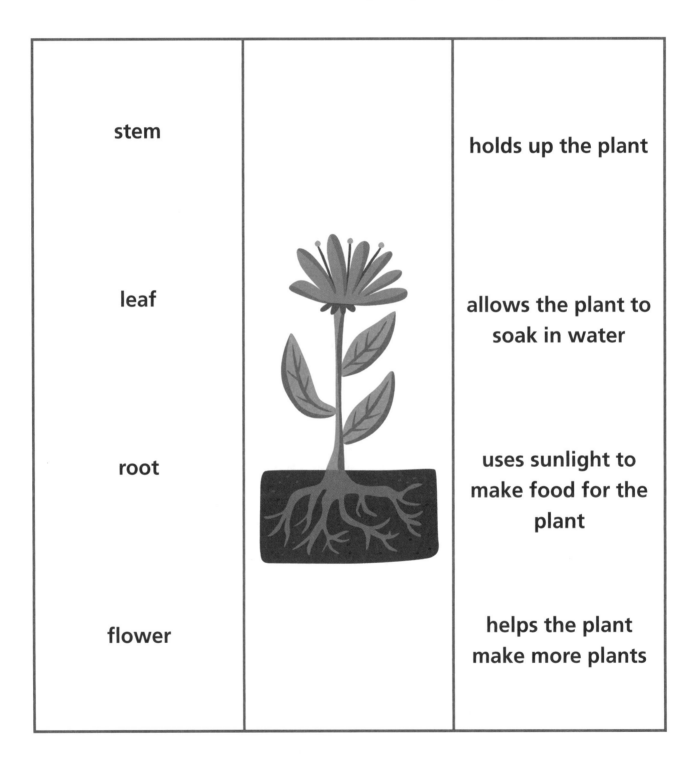	allows the plant to soak in water
root		uses sunlight to make food for the plant
flower		helps the plant make more plants

Then or Now?

Write **then** or **now** next to each picture to show when people did each activity.

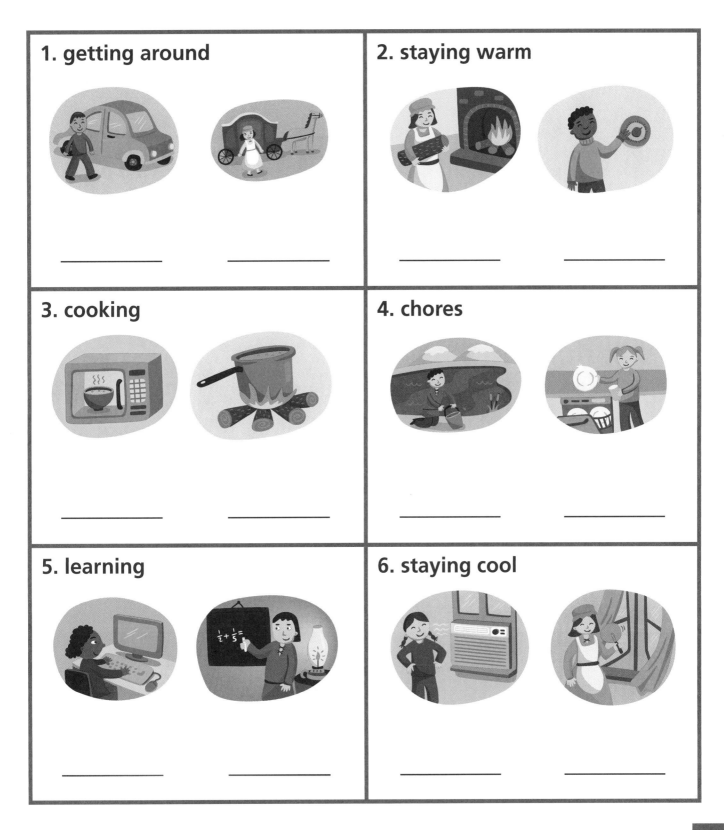

1. getting around

_____   _____

2. staying warm

_____   _____

3. cooking

_____   _____

4. chores

_____   _____

5. learning

_____   _____

6. staying cool

_____   _____

Mixed-Up Signs

Look at each group of signs. Color the sign with the greatest number green.
Color the sign with the lowest number yellow.

1.   7,039   4,290   9,099   **2.**   2,083   5,257   1,008

3.   8,620   8,320   8,220   **4.**   3,273   3,115   3,151

5.   4,982   2,273   8,893   **6.**   6,123   5,918   5,981

Synonym Search

Choose the word from the word bank that means the same as the underlined word in each sentence. Write the word on the line.

soon	store	wonderful	greatest
stay	stuck	party	scared
	eat	interesting	

1. You are my <u>best</u> friend! _____

2. Will you come with me to the <u>market</u> today? _____

3. I have to buy food for tonight's <u>celebration</u>. _____

4. We can make a <u>magnificent</u> cherry pie. _____

5. Don't be <u>frightened</u> if the bus comes late. _____

6. We will not be <u>stranded</u> at the bus stop. _____

7. A bus will pick us up <u>shortly</u>. _____

8. Ask your mom if you can <u>remain</u> at my house until the party is over.

_____

9. We can watch a <u>fascinating</u> movie about amusement parks!

_____

10. I'm sure everyone will <u>devour</u> the cherry pie! _____

Adam's Birthday Party

Adam woke up sad on his birthday. The weatherman had predicted a terrible storm for the day. Adam's parents thought it would be safer to cancel his beach party celebration and have it on another day.

Around lunchtime, Adam took a walk on the beach with his dad. They brought their umbrellas and listened to the rain falling on the sand. "I think the storm is getting worse," said his dad. "Let's go home now."

When they got to the house, all the lights were out and it seemed no one was home. Suddenly everyone yelled, "Surprise!" Adam could not believe it! All his friends and family were there. Everyone was wearing beach clothes. They had beach balls, towels, and beach food. Adam's parents had secretly moved the party indoors! Adam's sad birthday became a happy birthday.

Answer the questions about the story.

1. How did Adam feel at the beginning of the story? Why?

_____

2. What happened in the story that changed the way Adam felt?

_____

3. What characters are in the story besides Adam?

_____

Magnetic Motorcycle?

Look at the motorcycle below. Place a check next to each part of the motorcycle that would be attracted to a magnet.

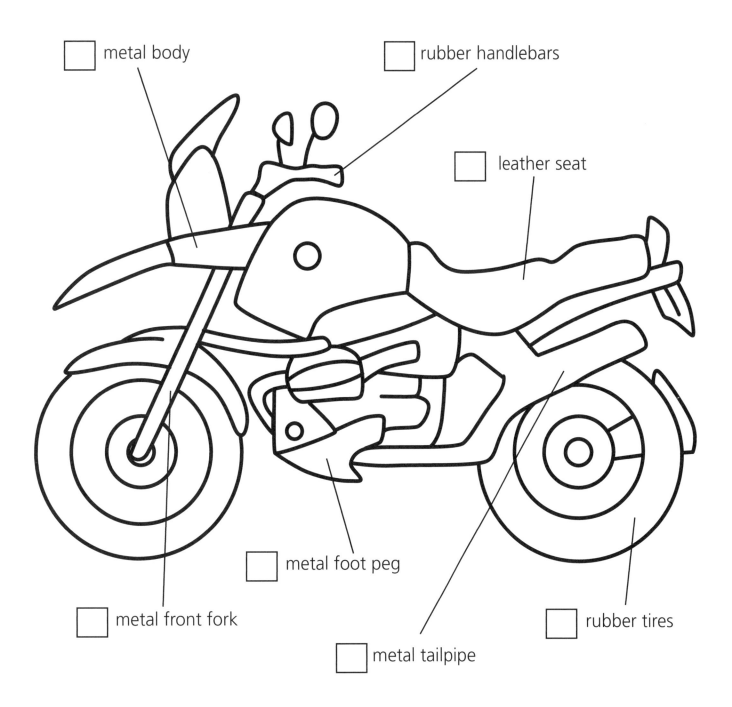

☐ metal body

☐ rubber handlebars

☐ leather seat

☐ metal foot peg

☐ metal front fork

☐ metal tailpipe

☐ rubber tires

Money Patterns

Look at the money patterns below. Draw to finish each pattern.

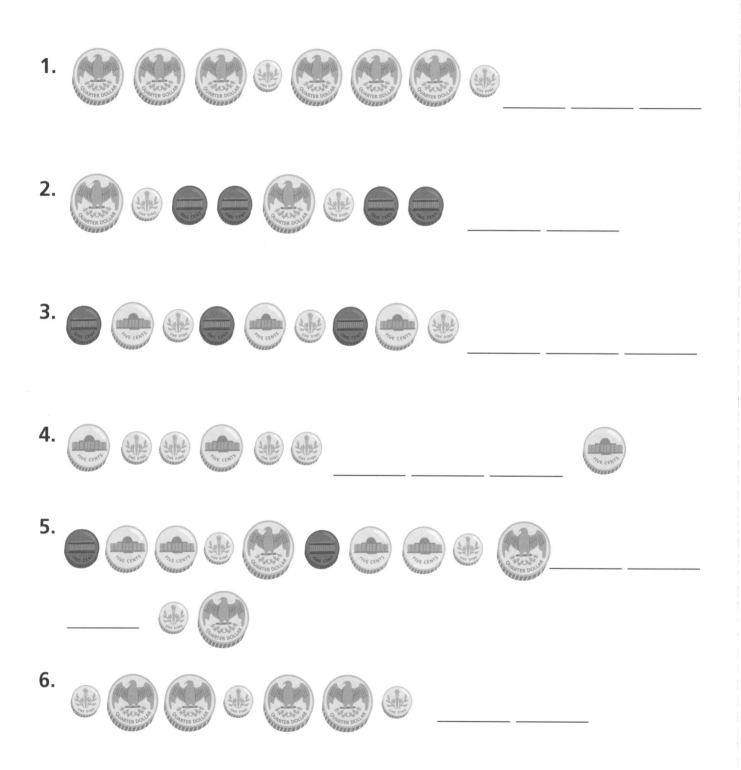

1.

2.

3.

4.

5.

6.

Follow Those Footsteps!

Figure out the pattern on the footsteps in each row. Then finish the pattern.

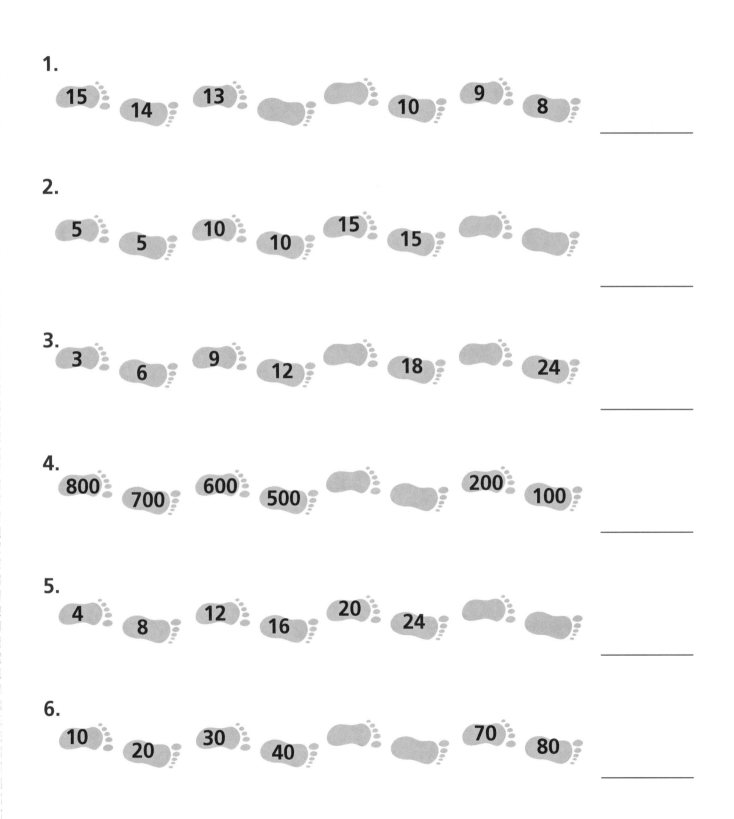

1. 15 14 13 ___ ___ 10 9 8 _____

2. 5 5 10 10 15 15 ___ ___ _____

3. 3 6 9 12 ___ 18 ___ 24 _____

4. 800 700 600 500 ___ ___ 200 100 _____

5. 4 8 12 16 20 24 ___ ___ _____

6. 10 20 30 40 ___ ___ 70 80 _____

Saturn

There are eight different planets in our solar system. Saturn is the second largest one. It was discovered in 1610. A scientist named Galileo saw it through one of the first telescopes. He saw an object in space with rings around it. These rings are what help people easily identify Saturn today. The planet was named after a Roman god named Saturn.

We have learned more about Saturn since it was first seen through a telescope. We now know that Saturn has many moons around it. More than 50 of them have been given official names.

Answer the questions about the reading.

1. When was Saturn first seen through a telescope? _____

2. How did Saturn get its name? _____

3. What are three more things that you found out about Saturn?

_____

_____

_____

Rhyme Time

Look at each picture. Write the name of the item. Then write three words that rhyme.

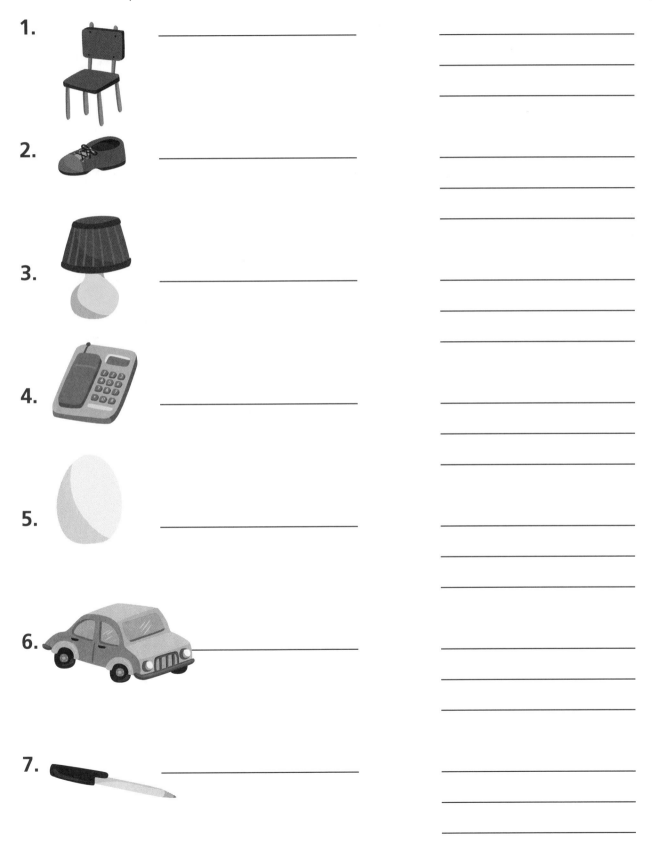

1. _____   _____
                              _____
                              _____

2. _____   _____
                              _____
                              _____

3. _____   _____
                              _____
                              _____

4. _____   _____
                              _____
                              _____

5. _____   _____
                              _____
                              _____

6. _____   _____
                              _____
                              _____

7. _____   _____
                              _____
                              _____

Mixing Paints

Mixing paints to make art can be fun. Three basic colors can be mixed to create all other colors. These basic colors are red, blue and yellow. They are called primary colors. You cannot make them by mixing other colors.

Mixing primary colors together makes secondary colors. Blue and red make purple. Red and yellow make orange. Blue and yellow make green.

By mixing primary colors in different ways, almost any color can be made. You can experiment with paints, colored pencils, or even crayons to get different results!

Answer the questions about the reading.

1. What are the primary colors?

_____

2. What color can be made by mixing red and blue?

_____

3. What color can be made by mixing blue and yellow?

_____

4. What color can be made by mixing red and yellow?

_____

Everything Has a Texture

The way something feels is called **texture**. Write two words to describe how each item feels when you touch it.

1. _____ _____

2. _____ _____

3. _____ _____

4. _____ _____

5. _____ _____

6. _____ _____

What Do They Do?

Describe the job of each person below.

1. teacher

_____

_____

2. librarian

_____

_____

3. mayor

_____

_____

4. store owner

_____

_____

Places, Everyone!

Look at each number. Answer the question. Write the answer on the line.

1. **829**   What number is in the ones place? _____

2. **932**   What number is in the tens place? _____

3. **306**   What number is in the hundreds place? _____

4. **240**   What number is in the ones place? _____

5. **157**   What number is in the tens place? _____

6. **381**   In what place value is the largest digit? _____

7. **189**   In what place value is the smallest digit? _____

8. **276**   In what place value is the largest digit? _____

9. **920**   In what place value is a 0? _____

10. **993**   In what place value is a 3? _____

Opposites Attract

Draw a line between flip-flops with opposite meanings.

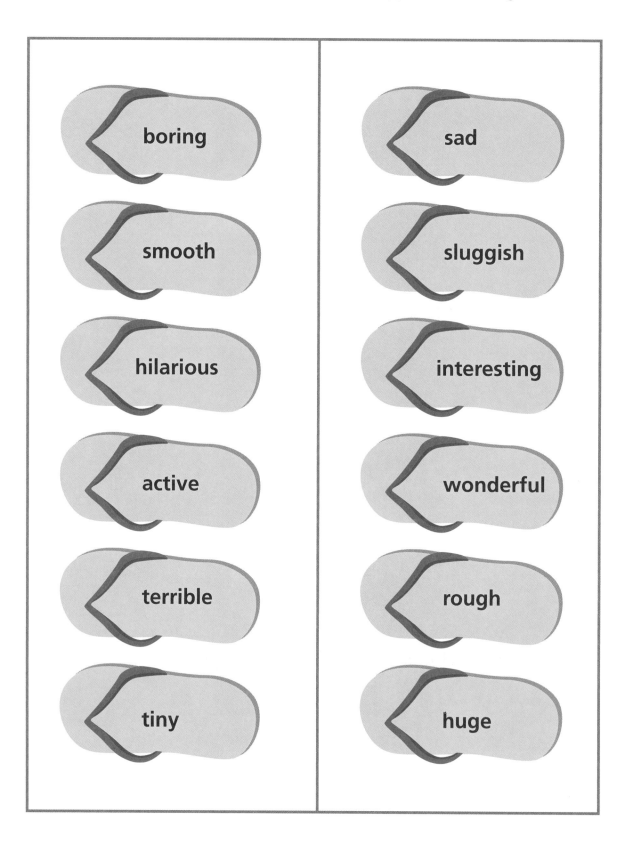

boring

smooth

hilarious

active

terrible

tiny

sad

sluggish

interesting

wonderful

rough

huge

One Animal, Two Animals

Write the plural word for each animal.

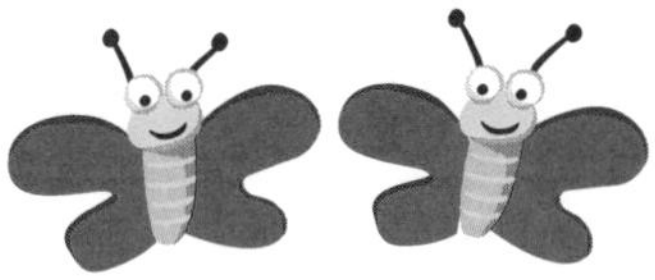

1. dog _____

2. fox _____

3. wolf _____

4. deer _____

5. sheep _____

6. goose _____

7. giraffe _____

8. rabbit _____

9. butterfly _____

10. pony _____

The World of Photography

You probably see dozens of photographs every day. You see them in magazines, books, and newspapers. You see them on television and on the Internet. And, of course, you see them in photo albums!

Did you know that the oldest known photograph was taken in 1826? A French man named Joseph Nicéphore Niépce took a picture of a man walking with a horse. He also took one of a woman with a spinning wheel.

Photography has changed a lot through the years. Special films and chemicals were needed to take pictures in the past. Today we can use

 digital photography to record just about anything we see. But through the years, the idea of taking a picture to record an event or a special memory has always been the same.

Answer the questions about the reading.

1. What are three places we see photographs every day?

_____

2. When was the first known photograph taken?

_____

3. What kind of photography can people use today?

_____

Celebrate Family

Think of two favorite events that you celebrate with your family. In the picture frames below, draw yourself celebrating these events with your family. Write a sentence to describe each picture.

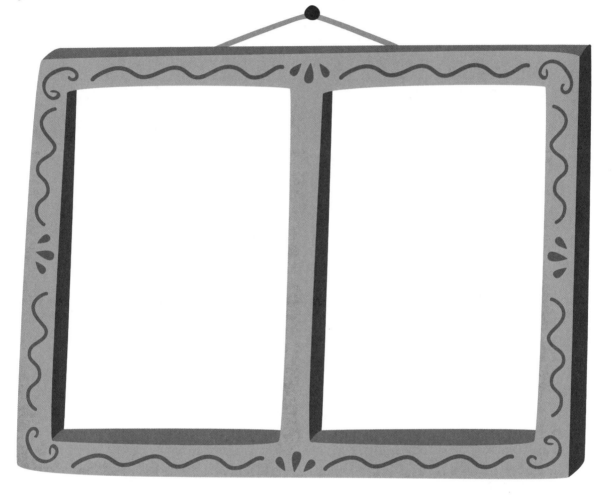

_____

_____

_____

_____

_____

Baby and Parent

Draw a line to match each baby with its parent.

Sounds Everywhere

Pitch is how high or low a sound is. Volume is how loud or soft a sound is. Write **high** or **low** to describe each pitch. Write **loud** or **soft** to describe each volume.

1.

A train whistle has a _____ volume.

2.

A whisper has a _____ volume.

3.

A scream has a _____ pitch.

4.

A growl has a _____ pitch.

5. Name two more things that have a high pitch. _____

_____

6. Name two more things that have a high volume. _____

_____

Communicating Through Time

Number the pictures to show the order in which they were invented.

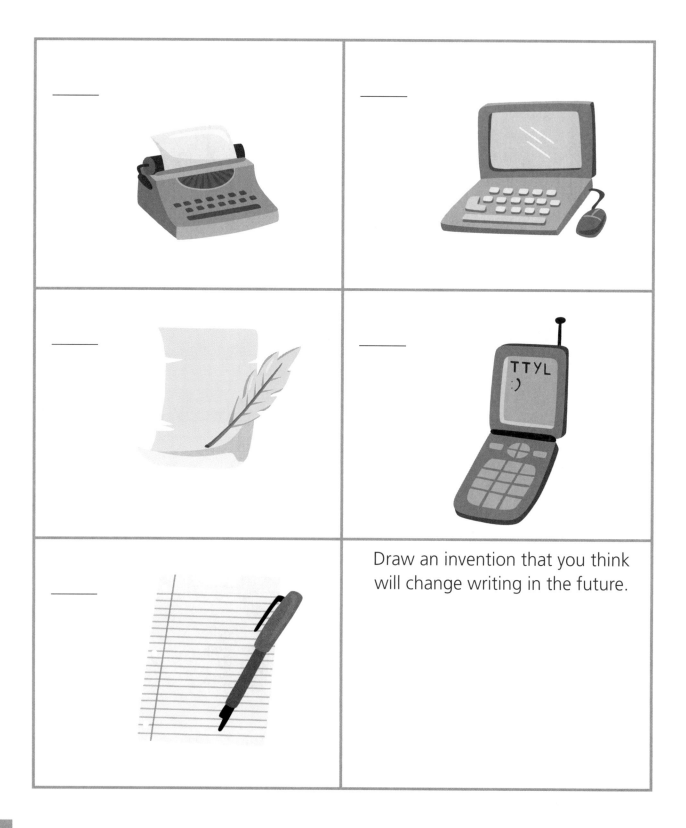

_____

_____

_____

_____

_____

Draw an invention that you think will change writing in the future.

Juicy Details

Use your own experience to write describing words to finish each sentence.

1. My bedroom looks _____.

2. My teddy bear feels _____.

3. My alarm clock sounds like _____.

4. My breakfast today tasted _____.

5. My favorite dinner smells _____.

Ellis Island

Ellis Island is a small island between New York City and New Jersey. In 1884, the Statue of Liberty was built on this site. It was a gift from France. It quickly became a symbol of American freedom.

Between 1892 and 1954, around 12 million people stopped at Ellis island. These people were coming to America from other countries. Records were kept of their names and arrival dates. Today, many of these people are honored on the Wall of Names. Visitors to the island can look up the names of family members who passed through the historic site before becoming American citizens.

Answer the questions about the reading.

1. Where is Ellis Island located?

_____

2. About how many people passed through Ellis Island before becoming American citizens?

_____

3. How are people who came to this country honored at Ellis Island?

_____

4. What famous American landmark is on Ellis Island?

Crossword Rhymes

Use the clues to complete the crossword puzzle.

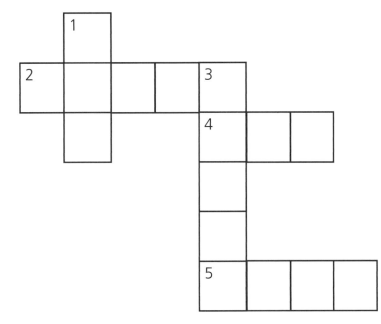

Across

2. Rhymes with gate - the word means **very good**
4. Rhymes with shout - the opposite of **in**
5. Rhymes with **fly** - another way to spell **hi**

Down

1. Rhymes with **sigh** - the word means to **weep**
3. Rhymes with **puff** - the word means very **strong**

Guess the Price

Estimate the price for each item. Circle the answer.

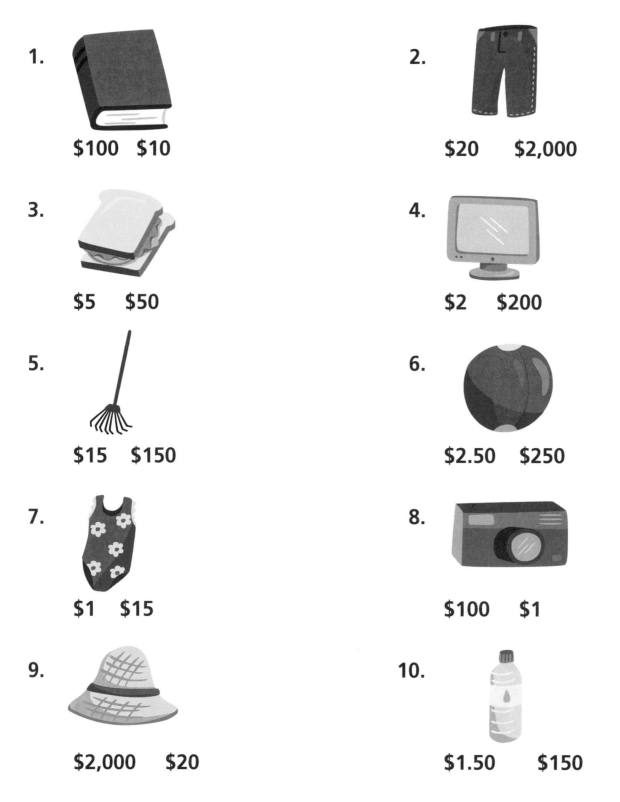

1. $100 $10

2. $20 $2,000

3. $5 $50

4. $2 $200

5. $15 $150

6. $2.50 $250

7. $1 $15

8. $100 $1

9. $2,000 $20

10. $1.50 $150

One Does Not Belong

Circle the object in each row that does not belong.

1.

2.

3.

4.

5.

Stars and Stripes

The flag of the United States of America may be one of the most well-known symbols around the World. There are 50 stars on a blue rectangular background in the upper left-hand corner of the flag. The rest of the flag is made of 13 horizontal stripes. Six of the stripes are white and seven are red.

The design of the flag has important meaning to Americans. There is one star for each of the 50 states on the flag. There is one stripe on the flag for each of the 13 original colonies. The flag has several nicknames, such as the Stars and Stripes and Old Glory. Many people hang the flag outside their homes to show their pride in America.

Answer the questions about the reading.

1. What do the stars on the flag mean?_____

2. What do the stripes on the flag mean? _____

3. What are two nicknames people use for the American flag?

_____   _____

4. What do you think a flag of your town might look like? Draw it.

Choose the Right Word

Complete the paragraph. Use the words from the word bank.

adventure	beach	short	great
night	tree	pirates	favorite	reading

My _____ thing to do is read. I love to read on the _____ . I read in my _____ house in my yard. And I read before I go to bed at _____ . I love when I finish one book and can then start _____ about another new _____ . I have read about _____ and fairies. I have read long books and _____ books. Reading is _____!

Goods and Services

Goods are things people can own. Services are things people can do for others. Suppose you spend the day with your family at an amusement park. Write some goods and services that people can provide for you at the park.

Goods	Services

The Telephone Through Time

Think about how telephones have changed since they were invented.
Number the events in the correct order.

_____ People began to have more than one telephone in their homes.

_____ Written messages can be sent through cell phones.

_____ Telephone signals can be sent through the air for cell phone service.

_____ Buttons replaced dials on many telephones.

_____ All telephone calls had to be placed by an operator.

_____ Telephone lines were connected across the country.

_____ The first telephone call was made.

Proteins for Your Body

Protein is something your body needs. It keeps you healthy. How can you get the protein you need? Eating meats such as beef, chicken, and fish are a good way to get it. Also try eggs, nuts, and beans. After you eat, your stomach helps to break down proteins and make them into chemicals that your body can use. Your muscles, hair, organs, and nails are all made stronger by different proteins. Protein is even used to make parts of your blood that keep your body healthy.

So listen the next time someone tells you to finish your eggs or to eat your chicken. Your body will thank you!

Answer the questions about the reading.

1. What are some foods you can eat to get protein?

_____

2. What are some body parts that are helped by eating protein?

_____

3. What part of your body helps to break down proteins into something your body can use?

_____

The Forgetful Squirrel

Sammy the squirrel had trouble remembering many things. He would often forget the names of other squirrels. He would forget how to get home. He would forget when he was supposed to meet friends. The most forgetful thing he ever did was to misplace all the nuts he had gathered and stored for the coming winter.

Sammy asked his close friend Leo for help, but they could not find the pile of nuts. Without his store of nuts it would be a very hard winter. Sammy would have to begin gathering the nuts all over again.

Leo helped Sammy so the work would go faster. Very quickly the friends were able to gather another large pile of nuts. One day Sammy found a big mound of dirt that looked familiar. He dug and dug and before he knew it he had uncovered his lost pile of nuts. Now he had more than enough for winter! He gave half of the pile to Leo for helping him when he was in trouble. It was going to be a good winter for both of them.

Write a summary of the story in your own words.

_____

_____

_____

_____

What's the Time?

Write the time that each clock shows.

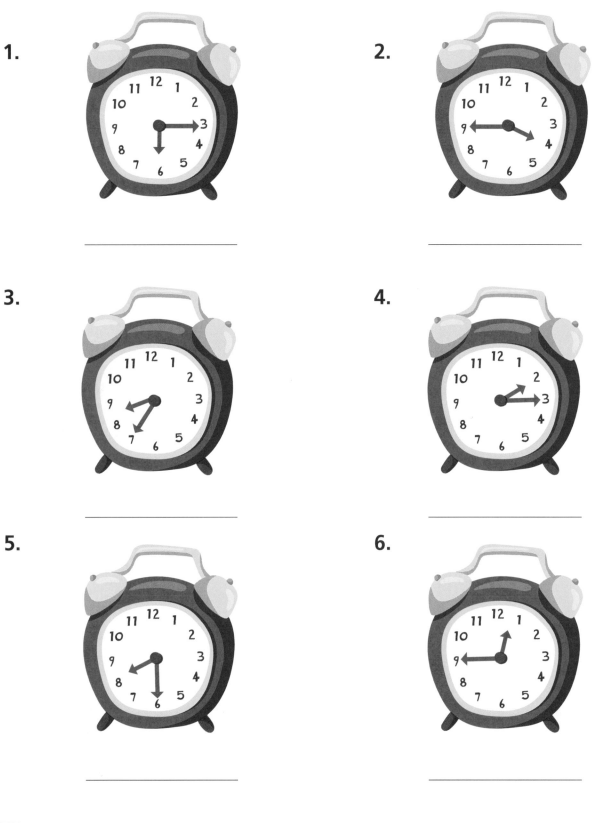

1.

_____

2.

_____

3.

_____

4.

_____

5.

_____

6.

_____

What Month Am I?

Solve the riddles.

1. I am three months after the second month of the year.
What month am I? _____

2. I am the third to last month of the year.
What month am I? _____

3. I come four months after November.
What month am I? _____

4. I come six months after August.
What month am I? _____

5. I am two months after the second to last month of the year.
What month am I? _____

6. I am four months after the fourth month of the year.
What month am I? _____

Around the World

The world map below has each continent labeled.
Use the labels to answer the questions below.

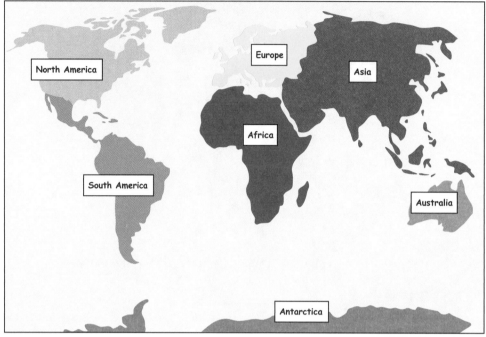

1. Which continent is the United States in? _____

2. Which continent is south of the United States? _____

3. Which continent is the farthest east on this map?

_____

4. Which continent is the farthest west on this map?

_____

5. Which continent is found between Africa and Asia?

_____

6. Which continent is the farthest south on the map?

_____

In Case of Fire

Preparing for a fire is something that can help save lives in an emergency. Lucy had learned this during Fire Safety Week at her school. Her teacher talked to the class about how important it is to find a safe way out in case of a fire. They looked around the classroom for safe exits.

When Lucy got home she told her sister and her parents what she had learned. They worked together to make a family safety plan. They listed all the ways out of the house and decided they would meet on the front lawn so that they could all find each other when they got out of the house. Lucy wrote down the plan. She made copies for everyone so they could study it and know what to do. Her family practiced a few fire drills, too. Lucy had helped her family, and everyone felt safer.

Answer the questions about the story.

1. Why is it important to have a fire safety plan in your home?

_____

2. What kind of plan do you have in your home in case of a fire?

_____

A Visit to the Zoo

Solve the problems.

1. Jake is meeting 15 classmates at the zoo.
Seven classmates have not arrived yet.
How many of Jake's classmates are at the zoo? _____

2. Jake saw 8 polar bears, 9 peacocks, and 7 zebras at the zoo.
How many animals did he see in all? _____

3. The zookeeper tells the class there are 21 flamingos. Jake sees only 12.
How many are missing? _____

4. Jake saw 12 monkeys outside and 18 inside.
How many monkeys did Jake see in all? _____

5. Jake spends $5.75 on lunch at the zoo cafeteria. He had a $10 bill.
How much money does he have left? _____

6. The zoo is open from 9 AM to 6 PM today.
How many hours is the zoo open today? _____

Solid, Liquid, and Gas

Look at each picture. Answer the questions. Write **solid**, **liquid**, or **gas** on the line.

1. What is the balloon? _____

What is inside the balloon?_____

2. What is the ball? _____

What is inside the ball?_____

3. What is the glass? _____

What is inside the glass?

_____

4. What is the pool? _____

What is inside the pool?

_____

Home, Sweet Home

Use the map to answer the questions.

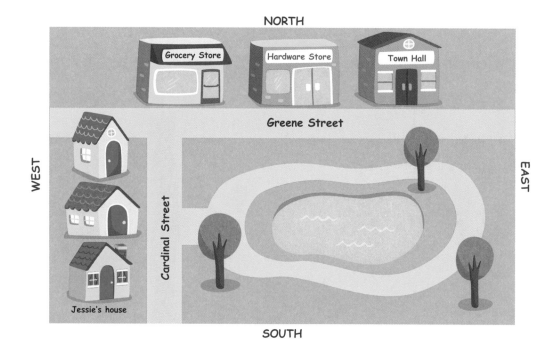

1. Jessie's home is _____ of the stores. (east, west)

2. Jessie must turn _____ on Greene Street to go to the stores. (left, right)

3. The grocery store is _____ of the town hall. (east, west)

4. The town hall is _____ of the hardware store. (east, west)

5. In which two directions must Jessie travel to get from the hardware store to his home? _____ (north, south) and _____ (east, west)

The Greatest Chef

Finish the word in each sentence. Write **–er** or **–est** on the line.

1. The great_____ chef in the world is a moose.

2. Mega Moose cooks a tasti_____ dinner than Leon the Lion.

3. Moose's desserts are the sweet_____ you have ever tasted.

4. Lion is a fast_____ cook than Moose, but he is not better.

5. Lion is also the funni_____ chef of the pair.

6. Which chef would make your meal happi_____ of all?

Art Camp

Write your own ending to this story.

Lucy had been excited to go to art camp. She loved drawing at home. She drew all the time. But when she got to art camp, she didn't love it so much anymore. There were so many other kids there. Everyone had to display their art in front of the room for the class to see. They even had to talk about the artwork they had done. Lucy was shy and didn't want to talk in front of a crowd.

Today it was time for Lucy to talk about her painting. What would the kids think of it? She nervously took her place at the front of the room.

_____

_____

_____

_____

_____

Measure the Animals

How many inches long is each stuffed animal? Use a ruler to measure.

1.

_____ inches

2.

_____ inches

3.

_____ inches

4.

_____ inches

5.

_____ inches

6.

_____ inches

Folding in Half

Look at the pictures in each row. Circle the picture that can be folded in half with both sides being equal.

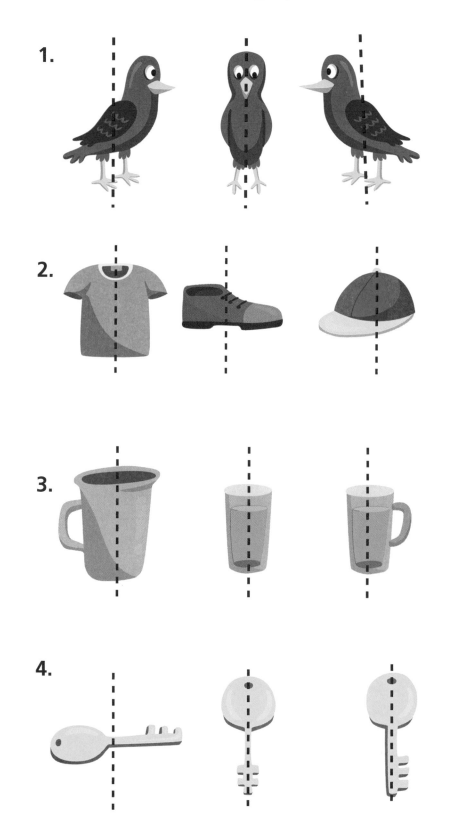

1.

2.

3.

4.

Cafeteria Times

Solve the problems. Show your work.

1. Jessie eats 2 slices of bread with lunch every day. How many slices will he eat in 5 days? _____

2. Each class bought 3 cupcakes from the bake sale. There are 4 classes. How many cupcakes were sold at the bake sale? _____

3. For each of the past 5 weeks, 3 different students in Mrs. Lee's class have forgotten to bring a snack to school. How many students have forgotten a snack in the past 5 weeks? _____

4. The school sells about 24 cartons of milk during every lunch period. How many cartons would the school sell in two lunch periods? _____

Word Search

Find each word below in the word puzzle.

> adjective   verb   noun   capital
> period   exclamation   comma

```
A  X  R  Q  I  Y  O  S  Q  N  U  O
D  T  C  O  M  M  A  P  X  S  W  B
J  G  E  A  L  P  C  P  O  U  M  E
E  X  C  L  A  M  A  T  I  O  N  R
C  D  G  B  E  Y  P  E  R  I  O  D
T  S  E  U  T  D  I  O  N  C  U  H
I  J  P  Z  A  M  T  U  T  O  N  D
V  E  R  B  J  N  A  R  W  I  V  T
E  O  K  R  H  D  L  U  G  S  D  A
```

In the Middle

Write your own middle part to this story.

    It seemed that the only thing Lacy's new puppy liked to do was jump up and down and bark. Lacy tried everything to make Rover calm down, but so far nothing was working. She had to try something new.

_____

_____

_____

_____

_____

    "Wow, you've really gotten that dog under control, Lacy," said Mom. "I'm proud of you. Your plan really worked!"

Predator or Prey?

A predator is an animal that hunts for food. The food it finds is called its prey.

Look at each pair of animals. Which do you think is the predator? Circle its picture.

1.

2.

3.

4.

5.

Around the City

Use the map to answer the questions.

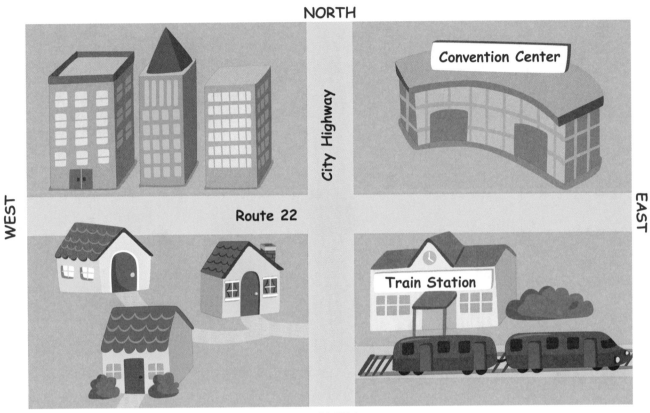

1. Maddie is in the convention center. In which direction should she go to get to the train station? _____

2. Maddie works in a city high-rise building. In which direction must she go to get home? _____

3. Maddie drives down City Highway from the Convention Center. Which way should she turn to get home? _____

How Many Faces?

Look at each figure. Write the number of faces on each.

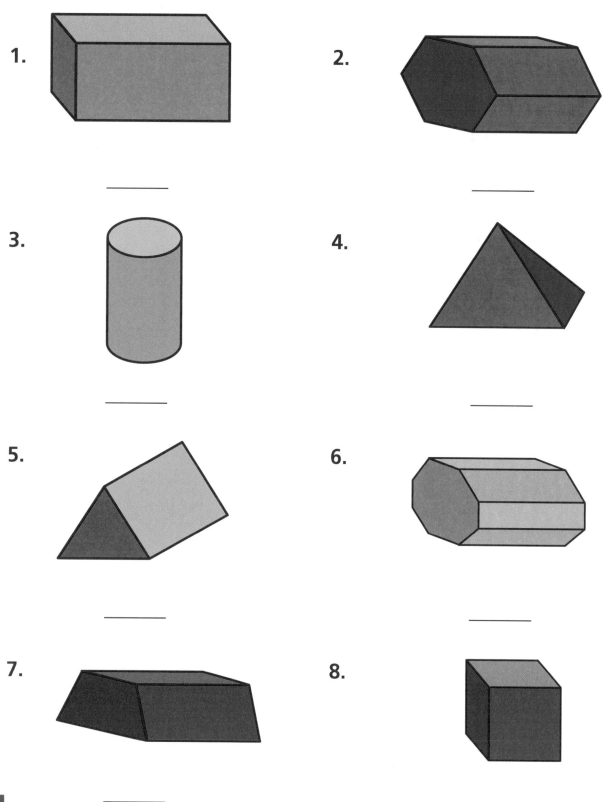

1. _____

2. _____

3. _____

4. _____

5. _____

6. _____

7. _____

8. _____

Matching Times

Draw a line to match each clock with the time that it shows.

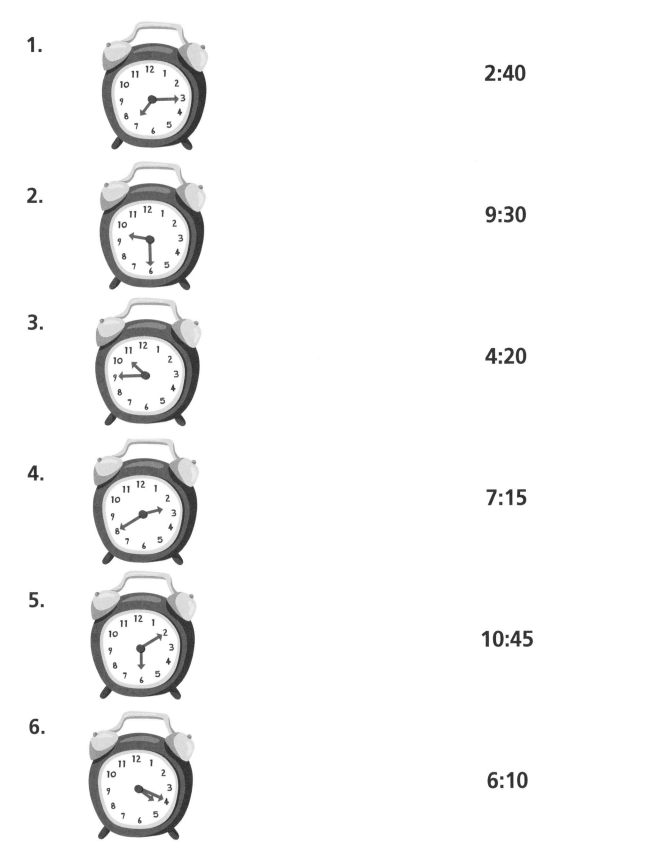

1.

2:40

2.

9:30

3.

4:20

4.

7:15

5.

10:45

6.

6:10

Babysitter Problems

Jessica loved having a baby sister. She looked out for her and tried to teach her new things. But Jessica got a little bit nervous when her mom and dad told her she could try to be a real babysitter for Maya.

"Don't worry, I'll be right downstairs cooking dinner," said her mom.

"What if I have trouble? What if she starts to cry? What will happen then?" asked Jessica.

"Don't worry. You will be fine. I just need you to keep her away from the hot stove. I think you're old enough to watch her," said her mom.

Jessica wanted to act grown up and help her mom so she played with Maya, did puzzles, and read books. After a while, Maya got a little cranky. She started to whine. She listened to Jessica less and less. "Oh, no," said Jessica. "What will I do now?"

"Dinner!" yelled her mom from downstairs.

"Phew!" said Jessica. "Saved by the bell!"

Answer the questions about the story.

1. Why does Jessica say, "Phew! Saved by the bell!" in the last line of the story?

_____

_____

2. What might have happened if dinner was not ready when it was? Write another ending to the story.

_____

_____

Draw the Time

Draw the minute hand and the hour hand on each clock to show the time.

1. 2:15

2. 12:30

3. 8:45

4. 7:20

5. 3:10

6. 6:50

When Will It Happen?

Read each sentence. Write the time on the digital clock.

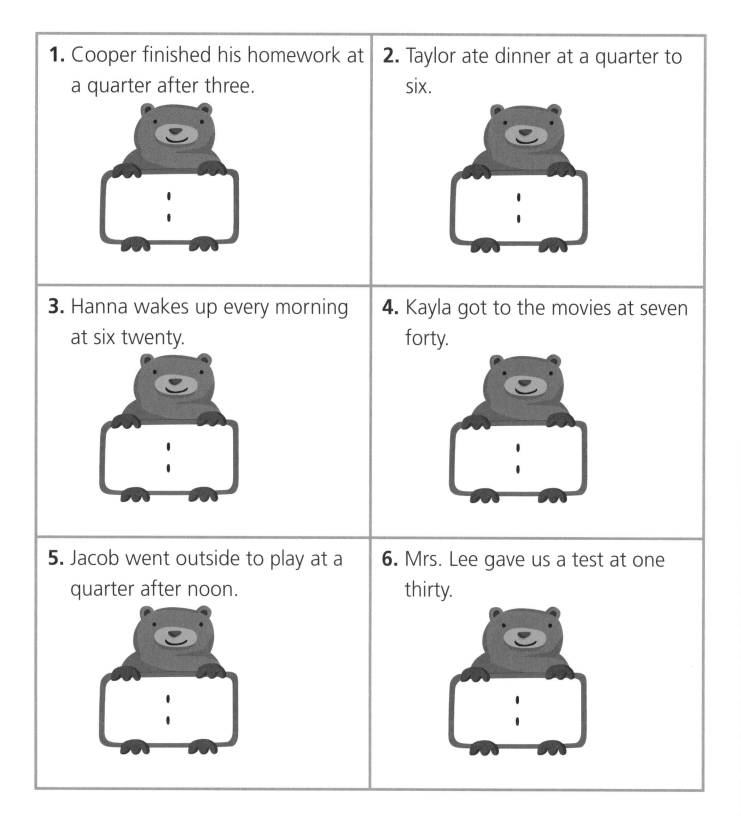

1. Cooper finished his homework at a quarter after three.

2. Taylor ate dinner at a quarter to six.

3. Hanna wakes up every morning at six twenty.

4. Kayla got to the movies at seven forty.

5. Jacob went outside to play at a quarter after noon.

6. Mrs. Lee gave us a test at one thirty.

A Letter Home

Dear Mom and Dad,

   This camp is terrible. Please come pick me up right away. The food is awful and I have not met a single cool friend yet. Everyone here is a much better swimmer than I am.
   The worst part is that I miss you. There is no one here to tuck me in at night or tell me a story when I feel lonely.
   If you pick me up from this awful camp I promise I will be cheerful and helpful at home. I'll gladly do any chore around the house. I'll do it all with a smile on my face. What do you say? Can you save me from having to do the three-legged race during next week's cabin competition?

Love,
Carlos

Answer the questions about the letter.

1. Who is writing the letter? _____

2. Who is the letter written to? _____

3. What are two describing words in the first paragraph that tell you that Carlos does not like camp? _____

4. What are three describing words in the third paragraph that give you a positive feeling? _____ _____
_____

What Do You Need to Live?

Think about the things that you need to live. Complete the sentences.

I need _____ because _____

_____.

I also need _____ because _____

_____.

And I also need _____ because _____

_____.

You Are the Family Pet!

What would it be like to be the family pet?
Write a short story to explain what it is like.
Answer these questions in your story:

- What kind of pet are you?
- What do you like to eat?
- What are your favorite activities?
- What is it like to be the pet in your family?

_____

_____

_____

_____

_____

_____

_____

_____

_____

My Favorite Library

Use the map to complete the paragraph. Write **north**, **south**, **east**, or **west**.

I went to my favorite library with my mom today. We got out of the car in the parking lot. We went _____ to get into the library. After I looked for books, we walked _____ to get to the playground. After I played for a while, we walked _____ to look in the greenhouse. Then we went _____ to get back to our car and go home.

Coin Matchup

Draw a line to match each number amount to the coins that show that amount.

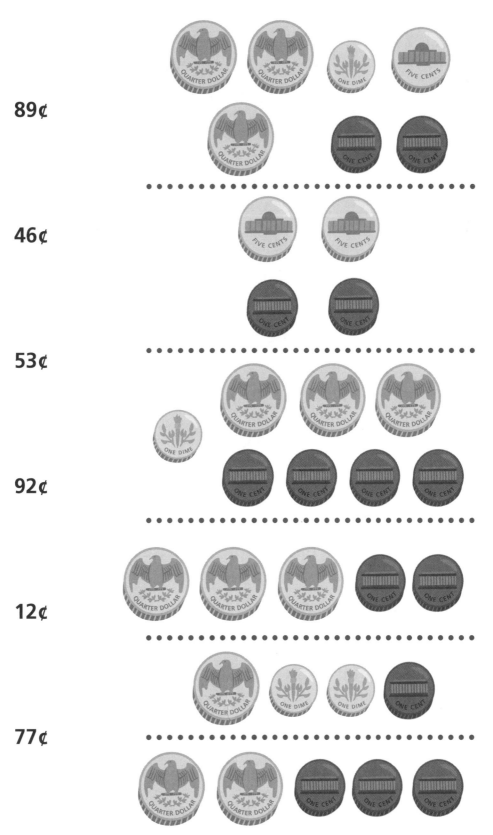

89¢

46¢

53¢

92¢

12¢

77¢

Maggie's Morning

Read the story below. You will rewrite the story as a play on the next page.

It was morning at Maggie's house.

"Are you all ready for breakfast?" her mom asked as everyone gathered around the table.

"I'm ready!" said Maggie's little brother, Max.

"Me too!" said Maggie's dad.

Maggie told her mom that she wanted to bring her lunch today because the school was serving sloppy joes. That was her least favorite lunch.

"Let me see what I can do about that," said her mom.

Maggie's dad asked her what she would be doing at school that day. Maggie told him that she had a math test. He asked if she was ready to do a good job on the test.

"You bet," said Maggie. "I studied for an hour last night. I'm definitely ready!"

Her mom said that was good, because the bus would be there any minute. It was all just another morning at Maggie's house.

Maggie's Morning Theater

Use the lines below to write the story on page 90 as a play. Write the name of the person who is speaking to the left of the lines.

_____

_____

_____

_____

_____

_____

_____

_____

_____

Our Presidents

Use the chart to answer the questions about the first five presidents of the United States.

President	Years
George Washington	1789–1797
John Adams	1797–1801
Thomas Jefferson	1801–1809
James Madison	1809–1817
James Monroe	1817–1825

1. How long was George Washington president? _____

2. What year did Thomas Jefferson become president? _____

3. What year did James Madison's time as president end? _____

4. Which person on the chart was president for the shortest time?

_____

5. How many people were president before James Monroe? _____

6. What year do you think the sixth president took office? _____

In the Bookstore

Number the book titles in alphabetical order.

____ Over the Clouds

____ Apples, Pears, and Bananas

____ Monsters Eat Garbage

____ Call Me Your Friend

____ Captain Tube Socks

____ Oh My Goodness!

____ Antarctica

____ My Favorite Foods

____ Silly Puppies

What's the Temperature?

Read each thermometer. Write the temperature on the line.

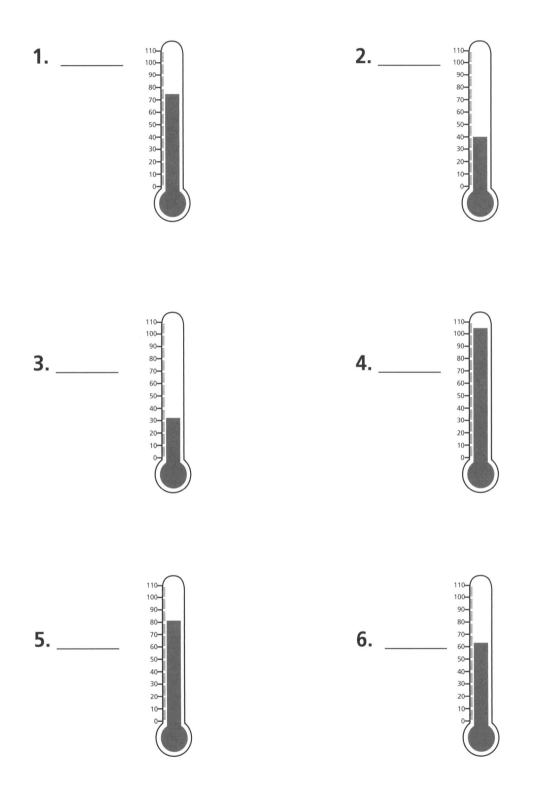

1. _____

2. _____

3. _____

4. _____

5. _____

6. _____

How Much Is Left?

Read each sentence. Count the money. Circle the money that will be left over.

1. Henry buys a sandwich for $3.45. What money will he have left?

2. Carrie buys eggs for $1.79. What money will she have left?

3. Christopher buys a drink for $1.25. What money will he have left?

4. Kim buys shoes for $10.50. What money will she have left?

Shapes Are Everywhere

Use the color key to color the shapes in the picture.

Color Key

Rectangle = yellow
Circle = brown
Triangle = red
Oval = blue

CIRCUS

What a View!

What great American landmark took more than 6 million years to make, is one mile deep, 277 miles long, and up to 18 miles wide? The Grand Canyon!

The rushing water of the Colorado River formed this great canyon. Over time, the water wore away layers of rock until large channels were formed. Large amounts of water melted into the river during the end of the last Ice Age. This made the water flow faster and wear down the rock even more.

The Grand Canyon is home to thousands of plants and animals. Today millions of people visit the canyon for its amazing views and for its interesting wildlife.

Answer the questions about the reading.

1. How deep is the Grand Canyon? _____

2. How old is the Grand Canyon? _____

3. How long is the Grand Canyon? _____

4. What caused the canyon to form? _____

5. What makes the canyon a popular place for people to visit?

_____

Word Mix-Ups

Unscramble the word in the suitcase. Then make 6 three-letter words using the letters in the word.

a n a t v i c o

_____

_____

_____

_____

_____

_____

What's the Story?

Look at the picture. Write a story about what is happening in the picture.

_____

_____

_____

_____

_____

_____

_____

_____

What Number Am I?

Solve the riddles.

1. I am an even number between 100 and 200.

I have a 5 in my tens place.

My ones place is between 0 and 3.

What number am I? _____

2. I am an odd number between 400 and 500.

The number in my tens place is half the number in my hundreds place.

The number in my ones place is less than 3.

What number am I? _____

3. I am an odd number between 700 and 800.

Add 3 + 4 to get the number in my tens place.

Subtract 2 from my tens place to get the number in my ones place.

What number am I? _____

4. I am an even number between 100 and 300.

All of my numbers are the same.

My numbers add to 6.

What number am I? _____

Scrambled States

Unscramble the underlined state in each sentence. Write it on the line. Make sure you capitalize the first letter.

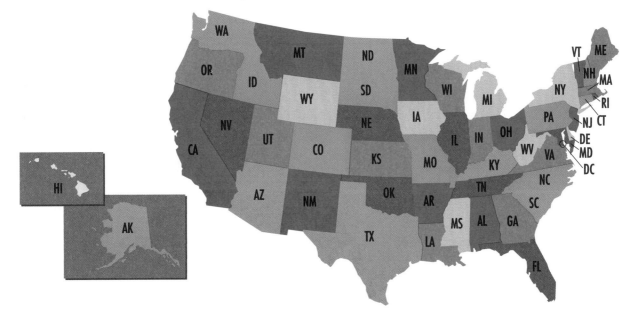

1. The state of <u>daflior</u> is in the south. _____

2. The state of <u>awiahi</u> is made of islands. _____

3. The state of <u>kaslaa</u> is the largest state. _____

4. The state of <u>icmgahin</u> has lakes around parts of it._____

5. The state of <u>xtase</u> is close to Mexico. _____

6. The state of <u>aaknss</u> is in the center of the country._____

7. The state of <u>agsonhiwnt</u> is north of Oregon. _____

8. The state of <u>dohre salndi</u> is the smallest state. _____

Useful Plants

Many items you use each day come from plants. Draw a line to match each item to the plant it was made from.

Look around your home for objects that could have been made from a plant. Do you see any? What are they? _____

Lovely Landforms

Use the pictures to answer the questions.

canyon   **mountain**   **valley**   **plain**

1. Which is the highest landform? _____

2. Which two landforms are on the lowest ground? _____
and _____

3. Which is the flattest landform? _____

4. Which two landforms are very rocky? _____ and
_____

5. Which landform might be the best for planting large crops?
_____

6. Write three words to describe a mountain.

_____ _____ _____

7. Write three words to describe a plain.

_____ _____

Reduce, Reuse, Recycle

Explain how you can reduce, reuse, and recycle things in your environment.
Complete the sentences.

1. I can reduce my use of _____ by _____ .

2. I can reuse _____ by _____ .

3. I can recycle _____ by _____ .

I Love a Parade!

My favorite event of the year is the Memorial Day parade in my town. There has been one on Main Street every year since 1921. This year we have a new mayor in town. He's a great mayor so far. He welcomed almost everyone as they came to the parade this year.

Memorial Day celebrates the people who have fought for our country. I think the floats and the bands in the parade make the day fun and festive for everyone.

My soccer team joined the parade this year. I think we made the best banner in the whole parade. We worked every Saturday morning for weeks on the banner. We finished it just in time. It has a painting of each of the members of the team and all of the coaches. When the parade was over we decided to put the banner up at all of our home games.

Write **fact** or **opinion** after each statement from the story.

1. My favorite event of the year is the Memorial Day parade in my town.

_____

2. There has been one on Main Street every year since 1921.

_____

3. He's a great mayor so far. _____

4. Memorial Day celebrates the people who have fought for our country.

_____

5. I think the floats and the bands in the parade make the day fun and festive for everyone. _____

6. My soccer team joined the parade this year. _____

At the Store

Read each sentence. Then look at the picture and choose the correct item.

1. Trevor has 2 dollars, 2 quarters, 2 dimes, and 2 pennies. Which item is the same amount? _____

2. Edward has 1 dollar, 1 quarter, 3 nickels, and 9 pennies. Which item is the same amount? _____

3. Kelly has 3 quarters, 3 dimes, and a nickel. Which item is the same amount? _____

4. Margo has 1 dollar, 3 dimes, and a nickel. Which item is the same amount? _____

5. Shari has 1 dollar and 5 dimes. Which item is the same amount?

_____

6. Leo has 4 dollars, 2 quarters, and 2 dimes. Which item is the same amount? _____

What Shape Will It Make?

Look at each drawing. Write the name of the figure that can be made by cutting the shape and folding it on the line. Use the figure names below.

cone   triangular prism   hexagonal prism

pyramid   cube   cylinder

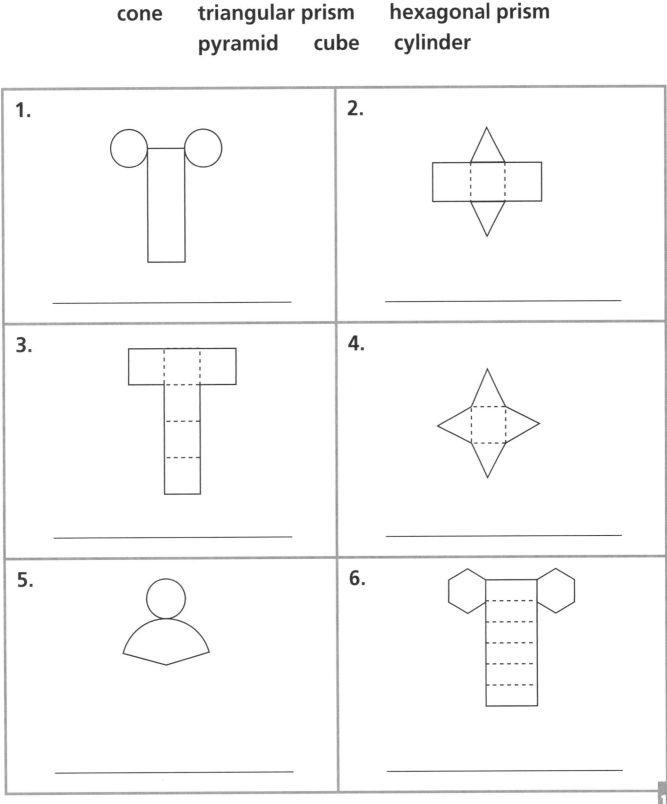

1.

_____

2.

_____

3.

_____

4.

_____

5.

_____

6.

_____

Frog Life Cycle

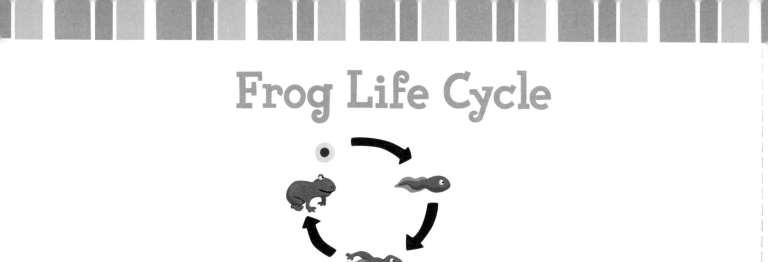

Baby frogs look very different from their grown-up relatives. When a frog egg hatches, a tadpole comes out. A tadpole looks more like a tiny fish than a frog. It has a tail for swimming and gills to breathe underwater.

After a few weeks, the tadpole grows legs and feet. As the legs grow, the tail shrinks. Lungs soon replace the gills for breathing, because the tadpole spends more time out of the water and breathes air. That's a lot of changes for one animal! The cycle that a tadpole goes through to become a frog is called a **metamorphosis**.

Answer the questions about the reading.

1. Why do you think a tadpole has gills instead of lungs?

_____

2. What happens to a tadpole as its tail gets shorter?

_____

3. Why do you think a frog has lungs instead of gills?

_____

4. What other animals do you know that go through a metamorphosis?

_____

Frog vs. Toad

What's the difference between a frog and a toad? Many people confuse the two animals, and it is easy to understand why. The animals look similar to each other! But there are a few differences.

The skin of a frog is wet and smooth. A toad's skin is dry and bumpy. Most toads are gray or brown, but frogs come in many different colors, such as green or even blue! Frogs have long back legs, while the toad's back legs are short. And the animals live in different places, too. Toads live on land. Frogs live in or near the water.

Next time you see a frog or toad, will you be able to tell the difference?

Write **true** or **false** after each statement from the reading.

1. Frogs live on land. _____

2. Toads have dry, bumpy skin. _____

3. Frogs have longer back legs than toads. _____

4. Toads come in many different colors. _____

5. Toads spend most of their time in or near water. _____

Just in Time?

Read the sentence. Then look at the time on the clock and answer the question.

1. The movie starts at 3:30. In how many minutes does the movie start?

_____

2. The soccer game starts at 12:00. In how many minutes does the game start? _____

3. School starts at 9:00. In how many minutes does school start? _____

4. The party started 15 minutes ago. When did the party start?

_____

Find the Change

Circle the dollars and coins to match the amount shown.

1. $1.35	
2. $2.50	
3. $5.20	
4. $1.85	
5. $6.25	
6. $1.55	

Reading a Map

Label the map. Use the words in the word bank.

stream	lake	factory	road
highway	railroad	bridge	park

Be a Mapmaker

Draw a map of your neighborhood. Show as many buildings or landmarks as possible. Be sure to include street names.

Finding the Food Groups

Circle the correct food group item in each row.

1. grain

2. vegetable

3. fruit

4. dairy

5. meat & beans

What Is Summer?

Summer and winter are very different seasons. Exactly how are these two seasons different? First, the weather in summer is much warmer than the weather in winter. Second, there are more hours of daylight in summer than in winter. Also, the trees look different in both seasons. Summer leaves are large and green. In winter, there are no leaves on many trees. They have fallen off and will not grow again until spring.

There are ways that these two seasons are similar, also. For example, they both have fun activities that can be done outdoors!

Complete the Venn diagram comparing summer and winter.

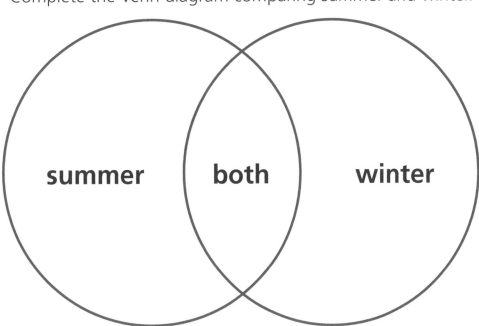

summer   both   winter

My Phone Book

In a phone book, names appear in alphabetical order by the person's last name. Write each group of names in alphabetical order. Remember to look at the second letter to put in order names that start with the same letter.

1. Sue Bottom
Becca Bear
Ricky Baboon
Janice Brown

2. Carrie Zebra
Marcus Zipper
Zachary Zap
Michael Zucchini

3. Hank Hippo
Harry Hockey
Jake Handshake
Carol Humor

4. Susie Social
Larry Saturn
George Street
Jessica Sleepy

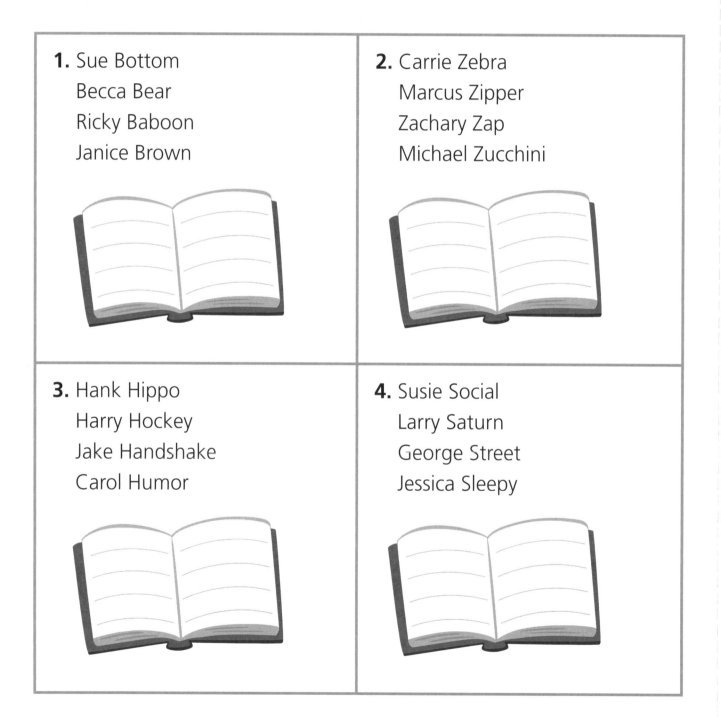

Shape Riddles

Solve the problems.

1. What shape has a rounded face and no corners?

_____

Draw one.

2. What shape has 6 sides and 12 edges all the same length?

_____

Draw one.

3. What shape has 8 edges with one side a square and the others triangles?

_____

Draw one.

4. What do you call a shape made of 2 cubes side by side?

_____

Draw one.

Make It Shorter!

A contraction is a shorter way to write two words. An apostrophe takes the place of a missing letter or letters. Draw a line from each word to its contraction.

she will	don't
they are	wouldn't
we will	she'll
do not	you're
he is	should've
you are	he's
would not	I'll
can not	they're
I will	we'll
should have	can't

Take a Good Guess

Sophie loved to snoop around the house before her birthday and look for her presents. Sophie peeked in her mom's closet and found what looked like a box for clothing. She peeked inside. There was another box inside the clothing box! She snooped some more and found three more boxes, each one smaller than the one before it. "What is happening here?" she whispered to herself.

Sophie had all five boxes spread out on the floor of her mom's bedroom. Just as she was opening the last one, Sophie was caught in the act.

"What are you doing?" asked her mom as she entered the room.

"Oh, no," said Sophie. She reached into the box and found a tiny outfit meant for a doll. Sophie's eyes widened. "Clothing for a Daisy Doll!" she screamed. "Am I getting a Daisy Doll for my birthday?" she asked.

"I'll never tell!" said her mom with a smile as she walked out of the room.

Answer the questions about the story.

1. Why do you think Sophie's mom did not answer her question?

_____

2. Do you think Sophie's mom bought her a Daisy Doll? Why or why not?

_____

3. What do you predict may happen next in the story?

_____

Measuring Tools

Write the name of the tool that is used to measure each item below.

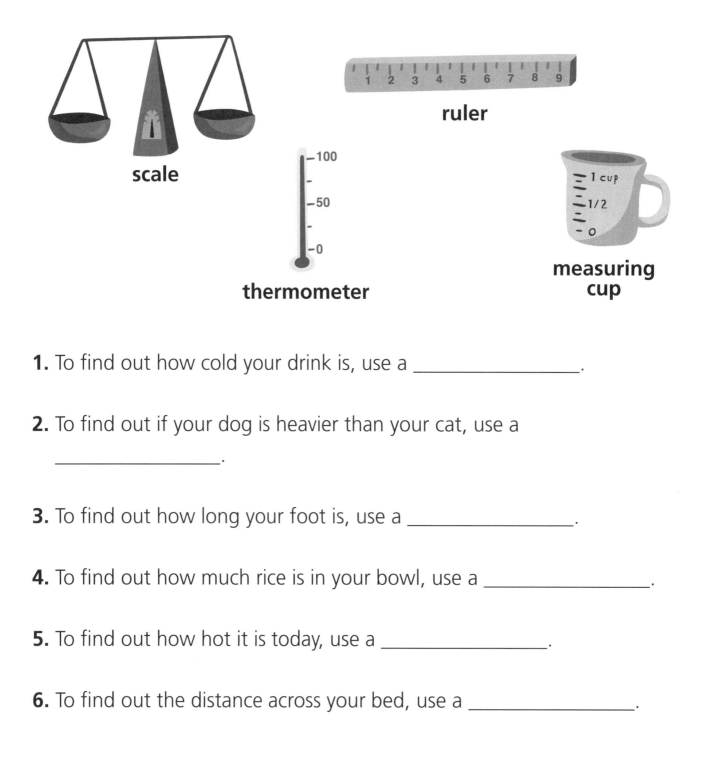

scale

ruler

thermometer

measuring cup

1. To find out how cold your drink is, use a _____.

2. To find out if your dog is heavier than your cat, use a _____.

3. To find out how long your foot is, use a _____.

4. To find out how much rice is in your bowl, use a _____.

5. To find out how hot it is today, use a _____.

6. To find out the distance across your bed, use a _____.

How Many Centimeters?

Use the ruler to measure the length of each item.

1. _____ centimeters

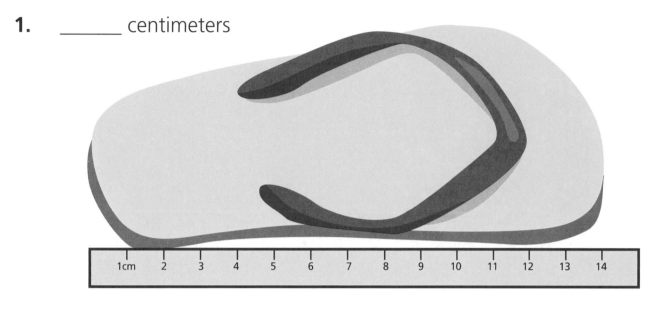

2. _____ centimeters

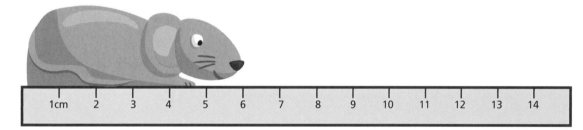

3. _____ centimeters

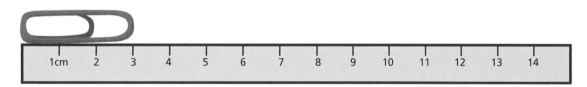

4. _____ centimeters

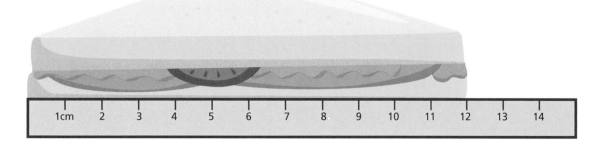

Have Some Pie!

How many slices of pie are missing from the whole? Write the fraction.

1.

blueberry pie

_____ out of _____ are missing. The fraction is _____

2.

apple pie

_____ out of _____ are missing. The fraction is _____

3.

pecan pie

_____ out of _____ are missing. The fraction is _____

4.

peach pie

_____ out of _____ are missing. The fraction is _____

5.

custard pie

_____ out of _____ are missing. The fraction is _____

6.

lemon pie

_____ out of _____ are missing. The fraction is _____

On the Move

The products we buy come from all around the world. What kind of transportation helps each product get to where it is going? Answer each question below by writing **truck**, **plane**, or **ship**.

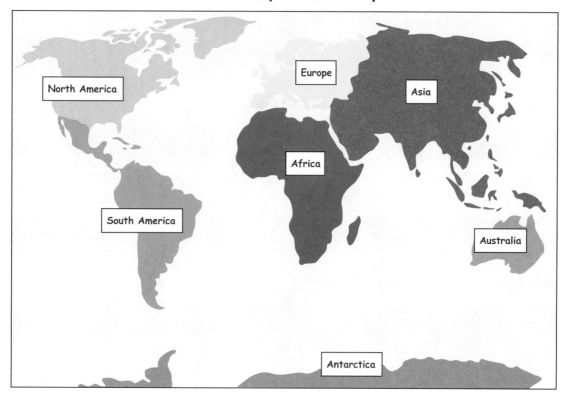

1. Bananas are shipped from Central America to Oklahoma. How do they get there?

_____

2. Paper is shipped from Oregon to Arizona. How does it get there?

_____

3. Cars are shipped from Germany to New York. How do they get there?

_____

4. Fish are shipped from Maine to Michigan. How do they get there?

_____

Let's Take Action!

Citizens can write letters to describe things in their community that they want to change. Think of something that you would like to change in your community. Write a letter to the mayor to describe the problem.
Try to suggest a solution to the problem.

Dear Mayor,

From,

Counting the Change

Add the money in each row. Write the amount.

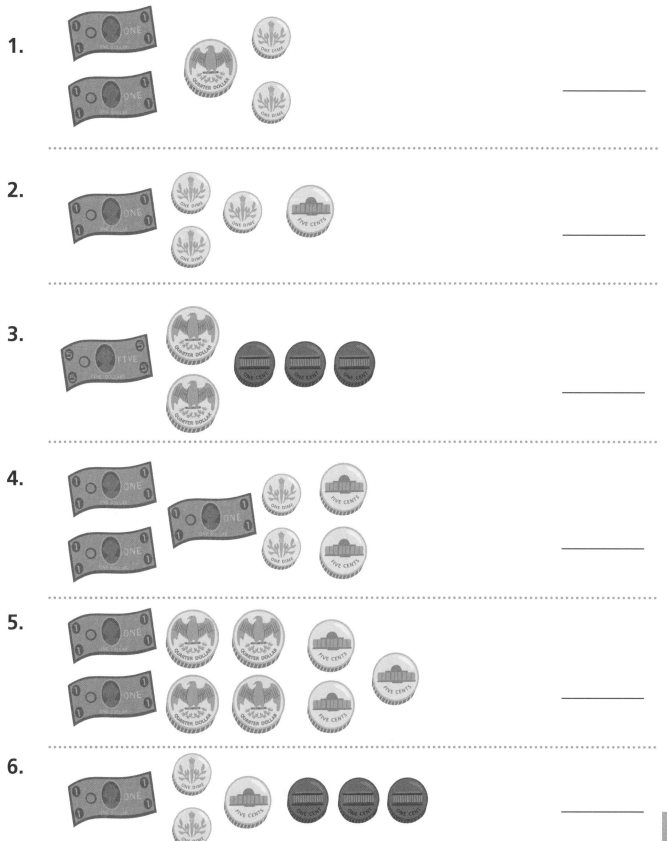

1. _____

2. _____

3. _____

4. _____

5. _____

6. _____

125

Number Riddles

Solve the riddles. Write the number on the line.

1. I am a three-digit number.
I have a 7 in my ones place.
I have a 2 in my tens place.
My hundreds place is twice the
    number in my tens place.
What am I?

_____

2. I am a two-digit number.
I can be made by adding 14
    and 15.
What am I?

_____

3. I am a three-digit number.
The number in my ones place
    is 2.
My tens place is twice the
    number in my ones place.
My hundreds place is twice the
    number in my tens place.
What am I?

_____

4. I am a 4-digit number.
I am made of 3 zeros and an 8.
What am I?

_____

Food Web

What does a bird eat? Many things! That is why a food web is such a complex thing. A food web shows what animals eat and what eats those animals. But each animal eats more than one kind of plant or animal in its environment. A food web has arrows that connect more than one living thing to several other living things it uses for food.

All food webs start with the sun. The sun gives energy to grass and shrubs to make them grow. In the food web below a grasshopper eats the grass and shrubs. A rabbit also eats the grass. A small bird eats the grasshopper, and a fox eats the rabbit. An eagle eats the small bird and the rabbit.

Draw arrows on the picture to show the food web described in the reading. The first arrows have been done for you.

Super Suffixes

Choose the correct suffix for each word. Use the suffixes in the box to help you.
Some words have more than one possible answer.

| -ize | -less | -ish | -ly | -able | -er | -ment |

1. self_____

2. understand_____

3. reck_____

4. paint_____

5. real_____

6. sudden_____

7. excite_____

Choose three words from above. Write a sentence using each word.

8. _____

9. _____

10. _____

Excellent Adjectives

Adjectives are words that describe nouns. Write four adjectives to describe each picture below. Think of the best words to describe each one.

1.

sand castle

_____
_____
_____
_____

2.

pie

_____
_____
_____
_____

3.

drum

_____
_____
_____
_____

4.

paint

_____
_____
_____
_____

5.

teddy bear

_____
_____
_____
_____

6.

scissors

_____
_____
_____
_____

Clara Barton

   Is helping people important to you? It was to Clara Barton. During the Civil War, Clara dedicated herself to helping soldiers on the battlefield. She was the first woman to be allowed in soldiers' camps, on battlefields, and in hospitals. Her work was a welcome help to the soldiers. She became known as the "Angel of the Battlefield."

   Clara founded the American Red Cross. It is an organization that helps people in need. Today the Red Cross helps victims of disasters, such as floods, earthquakes, and severe storms. It provides food, clothing, and shelter to people in need. The organization started with the good deeds of just one person. Thanks, Clara Barton!

Answer the questions about the reading.

1. When did Clara Barton begin helping soldiers on the battlefield?

_____

2. What nickname did soldiers give Clara Barton?

_____

3. What organization did Clara Barton start?

_____

4. What does the organization do today?

_____

Homework for Harry

Solve the problems.

1. Harry has to do 15 addition problems.
   He has to do 12 subtraction problems.
   How many problems must Harry do in all? _____

2. Harry writes 6 sentences for his science homework.
   He writes 12 sentences for his writing homework.
   How many sentences does Harry write in all? _____

3. Harry worked on his homework for 20 minutes in the afternoon.
   He worked for 30 minutes at night.
   How many minutes did Harry work on his homework? _____

4. Harry has homework 4 nights a week.
   How many nights of homework will Harry have in 2 weeks? _____

Which Is Heavier?

Circle the heavier object in each row.

1.

2.

3.

4.

5.

6.

Ounces or Pounds?

Circle **ounces** or **pounds** to tell which unit should be used to measure the item.

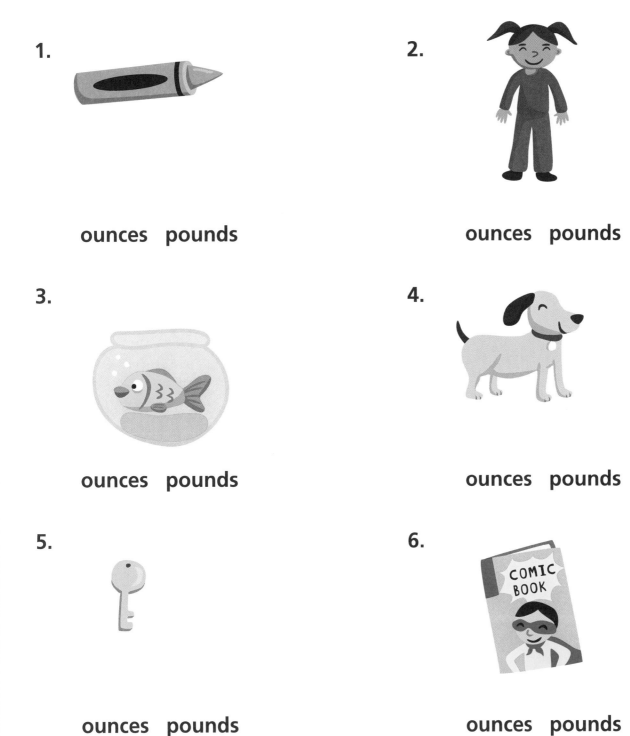

1.

ounces   pounds

2.

ounces   pounds

3.

ounces   pounds

4.

ounces   pounds

5.

ounces   pounds

6.

ounces   pounds

Fix It Up!

Rewrite each sentence correctly. Pay attention to spelling, capitalization, and punctuation.

1. I cant wait for sumer to be heer _____

_____

2. my Dog will be so happy to se me every Day? _____

_____

3. Mom says i can go to the Beach and to the Pool _____

_____

4. I Hop I can envite sum frends to com with me. _____

_____

5. we will Stay out and Play untul the sun gos down _____

_____

6. Thin we will play Again the next Day Two? _____

_____

Sorting the Recycling

Look at the pictures. Put the name of each item in the correct column of the chart.

Paper	Plastic	Metal

Food Groups

Write or draw a picture of your favorite foods in each food group.

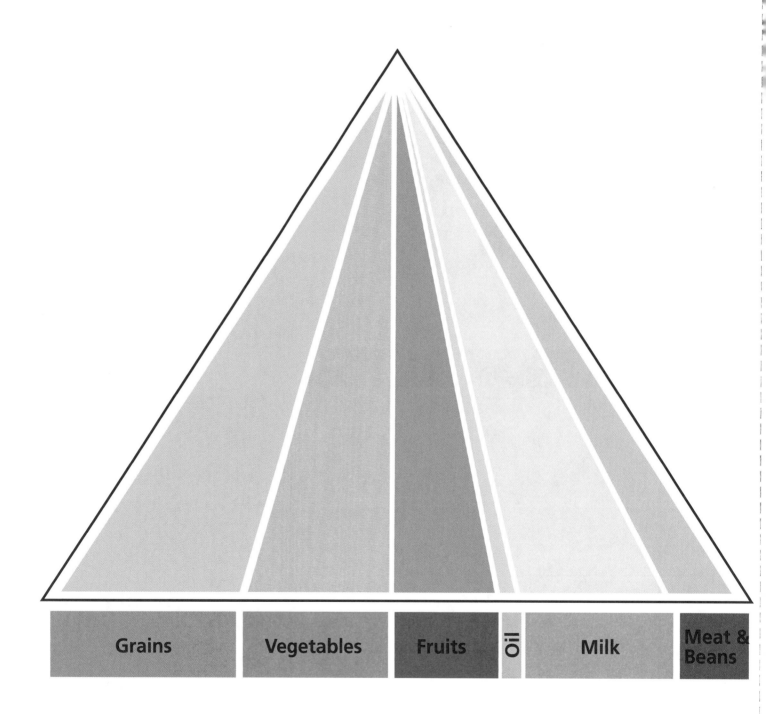

Grains   Vegetables   Fruits   Oil   Milk   Meat & Beans

Breakfast with the Family

Leo sat down to breakfast just like every other morning. The Menu Maker floated in front of him and he pressed the button for his favorite express breakfast: pancakes. The gadget floated back to its docking station. The stove began to rumble for a few seconds. Then Leo heard his favorite sound. The ring of the breakfast bell told him his pancakes were ready. A warm plate with his stack of pancakes floated back to him. He began eating immediately.

"Hurry up or you'll be late for school," said Leo's mom as she entered her own breakfast order into the Menu Maker. "And don't forget to order yourself some orange juice and a vitamin," she said. "Today is going to be another busy day."

Answer the questions about the story.

1. When does the story take place? _____

2. How do you know? _____

3. Where does the story take place? _____

4. Who are the characters in the story? _____

Estimation Station

About how many inches is each item?

Read the ruler and estimate to the nearest inch.

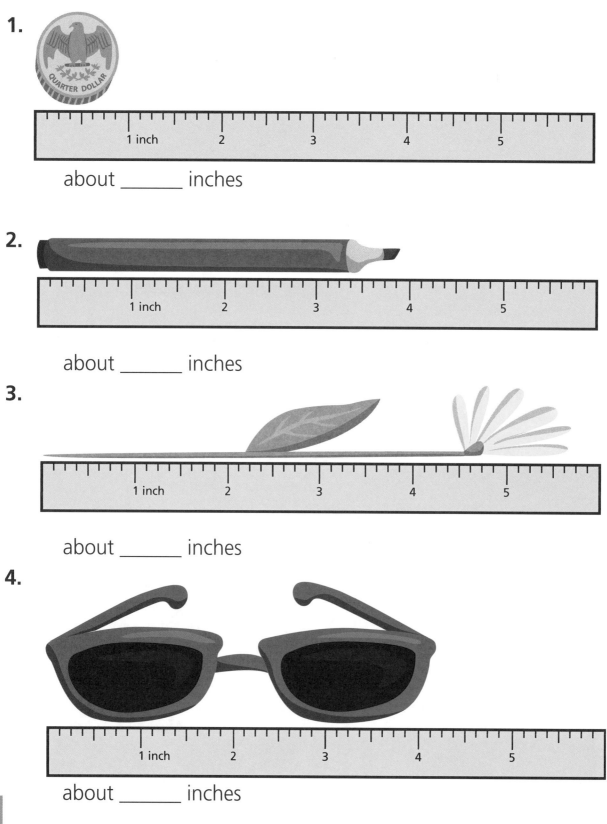

1.

about _____ inches

2.

about _____ inches

3.

about _____ inches

4.

about _____ inches

Making Fractions

Color in the number of parts shown.

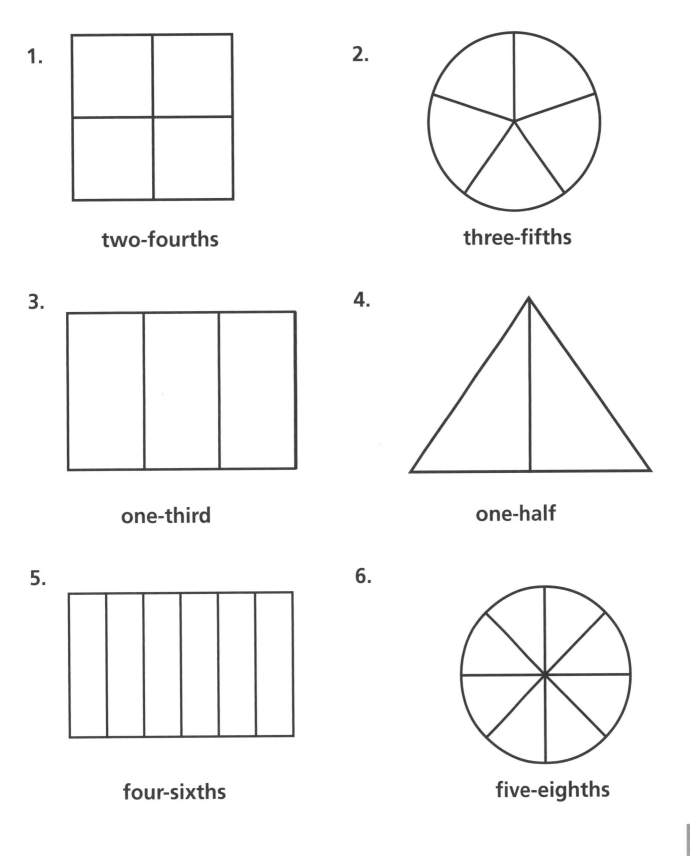

1. two-fourths

2. three-fifths

3. one-third

4. one-half

5. four-sixths

6. five-eighths

City Life or Country Life?

Write **city** or **country** on each line.

1. The word **rural** is another word for _____.

2. The word **urban** is another word for _____.

3. More people live in the _____ than in the _____.

4. A person is more likely to be a farmer if he or she lives in the

_____.

5. A crowded park is more likely to be found in the _____.

6. More animals are likely to be found in the _____.

Would you prefer life in the city or in the country? Why? _____

_____

The Big Concert

Write your own ending to this story.

"Buy your tickets today!" yelled Jason from behind the folding table in the park. His job was to sell as many tickets as possible to the town's big Forth of July concert. The money would go to buying a new playground for the town park. So far, Jason had sold more than 100 tickets to people walking through the park that day.

But then it began to look like it might rain.

_____

_____

_____

_____

_____

_____

Race Car Words

Color cars with action words blue.
Color cars with describing words red.
Color cars with nouns green.

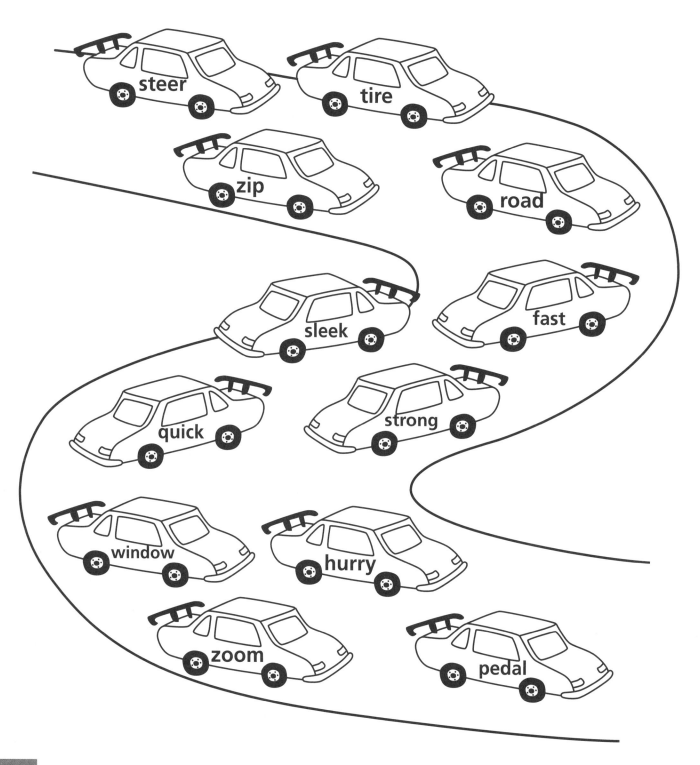

steer

tire

zip

road

sleek

fast

quick

strong

window

hurry

zoom

pedal

Put It in Order

Number each set of directions in the correct order.

1. Wash Your Face

_____ Add soap and lather it on your face.

_____ Fix the temperature of the water.

_____ Dry your face with a towel.

_____ Rinse the soap from your face.

_____ Turn on the water at the sink.

2. Write a Book Report

_____ Write about what you thought of the book.

_____ Choose the book you want to read.

_____ Read what you wrote to fix mistakes.

_____ Read the book.

_____ Think about what the book was about.

3. Check your e-mail

_____ Click on e-mails marked "NEW."

_____ Open your e-mail program.

_____ Log in your password.

_____ Write a response to your e-mails.

_____ Turn on your computer.

Make Your Own Fraction

Color in a fraction of each shape. Then write the fraction you made.

1.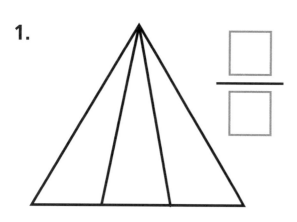

2.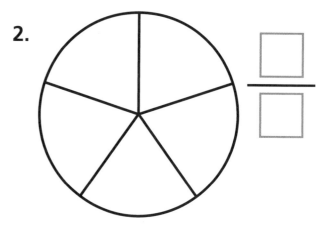

3.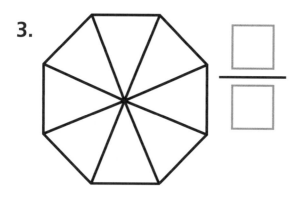

4.

5.

6.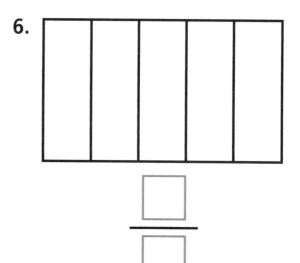

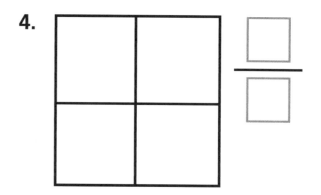

Game Time!

Use the graph to answer the questions.

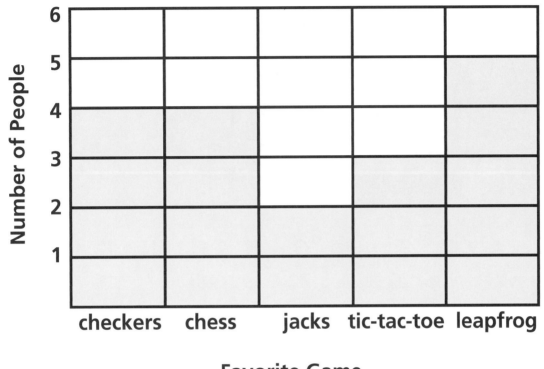

Favorite Game

1. How many people like tic-tac-toe? _____

2. How many people like chess? _____

3. Which game do people like best? _____

4. Which game do people like least? _____

Solve the Riddle

Use the key below to solve the riddle. Each letter matches up with a number. Write the letters that make up the answer.

A	B	C	D	E	F	G	H	I	J	K	L	M
26	25	24	23	22	21	20	19	18	17	16	15	14

N	O	P	Q	R	S	T	U	V	W	X	Y	Z
13	12	11	10	9	8	7	6	5	4	3	2	1

Why can't a bicycle stand up?

25 22 24 26 6 8 22   18 7   18 8
___ ___ ___ ___ ___ ___ ___   ___ ___   ___ ___

7 4 12   7 18 9 22 23
___ ___ ___   ___ ___ ___ ___ ___!

Staying Safe

Look at the pictures. Circle the things that help you stay safe.

How Can We Stay Safe?

Read each safety rule. Explain how it helps to keep people safe.

1. Rule: Cross the street with an adult.

Why? _____

2. Rule: Do not hit other people.

Why? _____

3. Rule: Wear a seat belt.

Why? _____

4. Rule: Stand back from the bus.

Why? _____

5. Rule: Wear a helmet.

Why? _____

Write the Fraction

Write the fraction for each picture shown.

1.

What fraction of pizza was eaten?

□
—
□

2.

What fraction of the lasagna is still in the pan?

□
—
□

3.

What fraction of drawers are open?

□
—
□

4.

What fraction of the slices were eaten?

□
—
□

Dan's Newspaper Delivery

Use the graph to answer the questions.

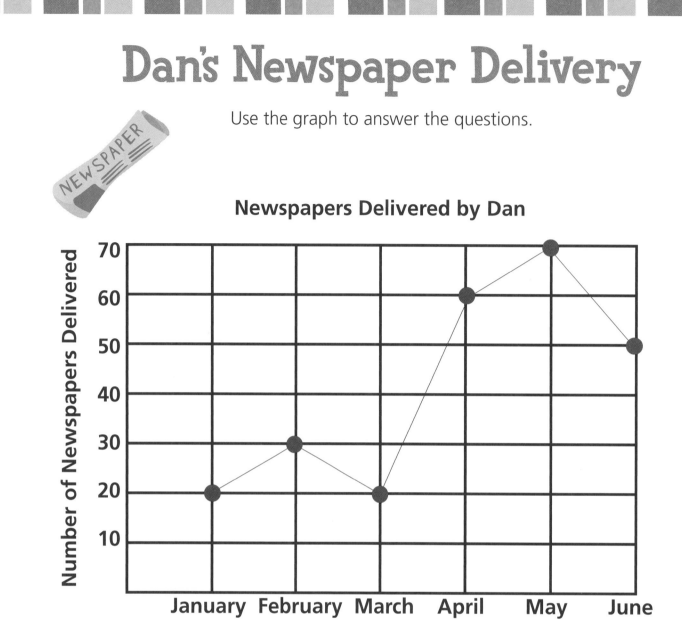

Newspapers Delivered by Dan

1. In which month did Dan deliver the most newspapers?

   _____

2. How many newspapers did Dan deliver in March? _____

3. How many more newspapers did Dan deliver in May than in June?

   _____

4. How many more newspapers did Dan deliver in June than he did in January? _____

Tally It Up!

Use the tally chart to answer the questions.

students who like yellow	ЖГ
students who like green	ЖГ III
students who like blue	ЖГ ЖГ II

1. How many student votes are shown on the chart? _____

2. How many students like blue? _____

3. How many more students like green than yellow? _____

4. How many more students like blue than yellow? _____

5. How many students in all like yellow and green? _____

The Pictures Say It All

Use the pictures to answer the questions.

1. How does Abby, the girl in the purple shirt, feel in the first picture?

_____

2. How does Abby feel in the second picture? _____

3. What do you think happened between the two scenes?

_____

4. What might happen next in the story?

_____

_____

The Same or Different

Read each word. Write a word that means the same.

1. playful _____

2. delicious _____

3. exhausted _____

4. terrified _____

5. funny _____

Write a word that means the opposite of the words below.

6. lengthy _____

7. complete _____

8. disgusting _____

9. happily _____

10. angry _____

Schoolhouse Riddle

Use the key below to solve the riddle. Each letter matches up with a number.
Write the letters that make up the answer.

A	B	C	D	E	F	G	H	I	J	K	L	M	N	O	P	Q	R
1	2	3	4	5	6	7	8	9	10	11	12	13	14	15	16	17	18

S	T	U	V	W	X	Y	Z
19	20	21	22	23	24	25	26

Why did the surfer wear a baseball mitt while surfing?

19   8   5   23   1   14   20   5   4   20   15
___ ___ ___   ___ ___ ___ ___ ___ ___   ___ ___

3   1   20   3   8   1   23   1   22   5
___ ___ ___ ___ ___   ___   ___ ___ ___ ___ .

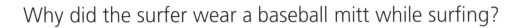

154

Tally and Graph

Use tally marks to show how many books each child has.

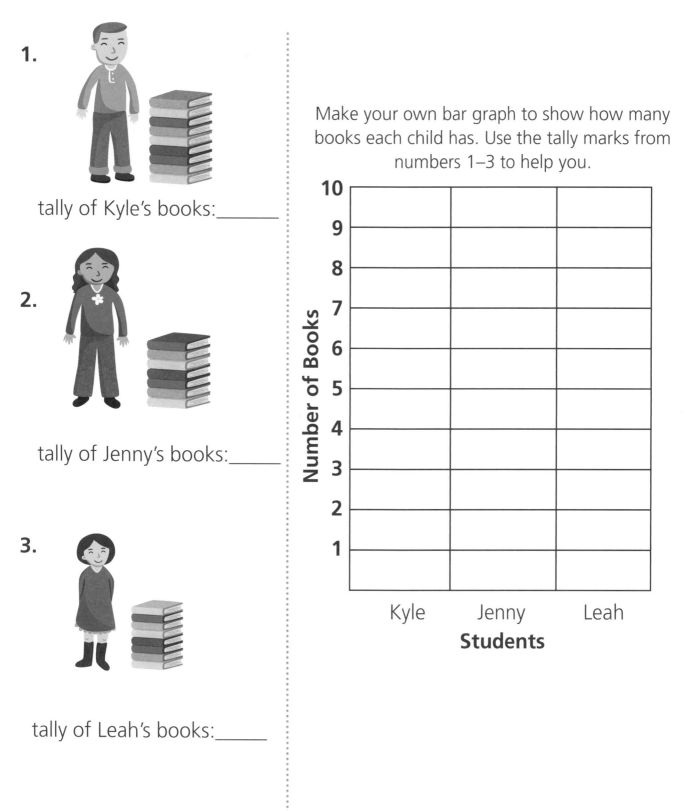

1.

tally of Kyle's books:_____

2.

tally of Jenny's books:_____

3.

tally of Leah's books:_____

Make your own bar graph to show how many books each child has. Use the tally marks from numbers 1–3 to help you.

Number of Books

10
9
8
7
6
5
4
3
2
1

Kyle   Jenny   Leah

Students

Balloon Math!

Add or subtract to solve the problems.

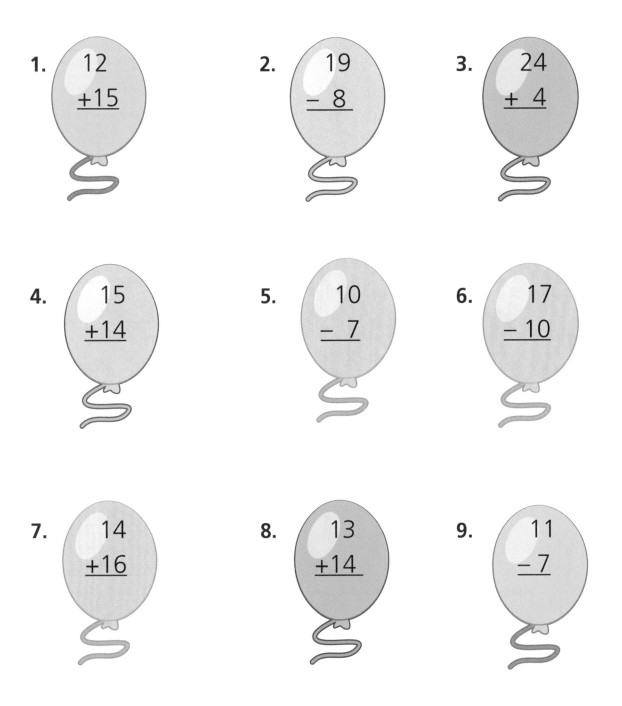

1. 12
   +15

2. 19
   − 8

3. 24
   + 4

4. 15
   +14

5. 10
   − 7

6. 17
   − 10

7. 14
   +16

8. 13
   +14

9. 11
   − 7

156

Dream Day

Imagine you could have a day when you could do whatever you want. Write about what you would do. Include as many details as possible. Then draw a picture to illustrate your day.

_____

_____

_____

_____

_____

_____

_____

Boomtown to Ghost Town

"Gold! There's gold in California!" This is what many people cheered in the 1800s when they found out gold was in the ground in areas of California and the American West. Anyone willing to dig in shallow streams in the area could find gold. They could sell it for enough money to support their families for a long time.

Boomtowns began to sprout up everywhere there was even a rumor of gold. Hotels, restaurants, and other buildings appeared almost overnight.

Then things began to decline. Not as many people were finding gold. Many boomtowns became ghost towns. People began to leave, until there was no one left. The days of the gold rush were over.

Answer the questions about the reading. Circle the correct answer.

1. What does the word **boomtown** in paragraph 2 mean?
   a. a town that has explosions
   b. a town that grows very quickly
   c. a town that has a lot of gold in it

2. What does the word **rumor** in paragraph 2 mean?
   a. a story that may or may not be true
   b. a story that is not true at all
   c. a story that is true

3. What does the word **decline** in paragraph 3 mean?
   a. to increase
   b. to decrease
   c. to not change at all

Jungle Subtraction

Color brown all the areas that equal 11.
Color green all the areas that equal 13.
Color red all the areas that equal 15.
Color black all the areas that equal 9.

159

Puzzling Addition

Circle three numbers across or down that can form a number sentence.
The first one is done for you.

12	14	7	7	9
7	3	5	8	0
5	11	2	15	9
1	9	10	6	16
6	2	12	9	21

Measuring Mass

Write the mass that is shown on each scale.

1.

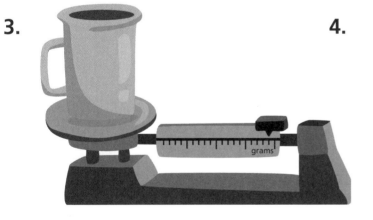

_____ **grams**

2.

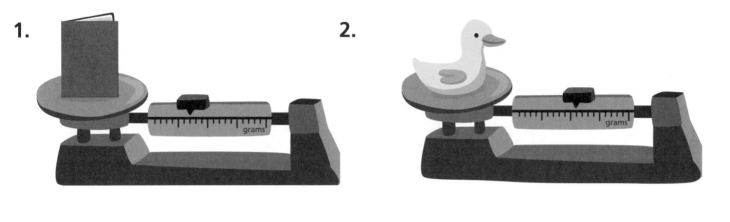

_____ **grams**

3.

_____ **grams**

4.

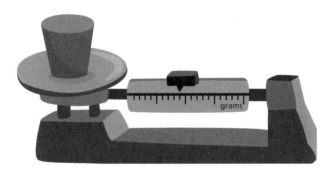

_____ **grams**

Letter from a Friend

Read the letter from a pen pal. Then write a letter to respond.

Dear Friend,

    I hope you are doing well these days. I am having a great summer. My family went for a week to visit my grandmother in Florida. It was hot there, but she has a great swimming pool. We spent a lot of time in it.

    Tell me what you have been doing this summer. How is your family? What friends have you seen so far? Tell me all about it!

    I hope to hear from you soon!

Love,

Me!

_____

_____

_____

_____

Number Matching

Draw a line to match each number sentence to its answer.

13 + 4	19
16 + 12	20
15 + 4	24
12 + 12	17
17 + 3	21
15 + 6	28

Subtraction Action

Fill in the missing number in each subtraction sentence.

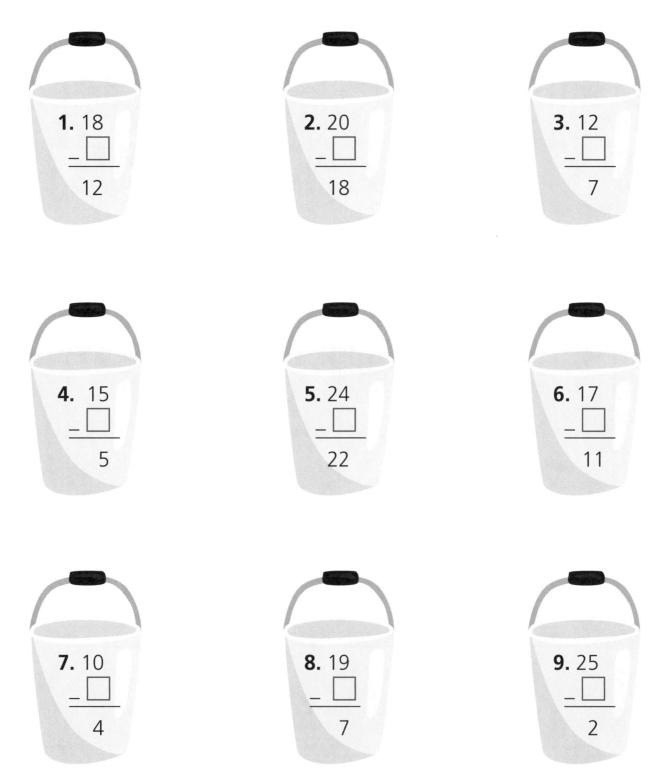

1. 18
− ☐
12

2. 20
− ☐
18

3. 12
− ☐
7

4. 15
− ☐
5

5. 24
− ☐
22

6. 17
− ☐
11

7. 10
− ☐
4

8. 19
− ☐
7

9. 25
− ☐
2

Adding Around Town

Color blue in the areas that add up to 15.
Color green in the areas that add up to 22.
Color gray in the areas that add up to 24.
Color brown in the areas that add up to 30.

14 + 1

12 + 3

10 + 5

16 + 14

15 + 15

17 + 13

18 + 12

18 + 6

11 + 11

18 + 4

16 + 8

15 + 7

12 + 10

11 + 13

17 + 7

Perfect Prefixes

Write the correct prefix before each word. Choose from the prefixes in the box.

| multi-   auto-   un-   non-   re-   dis-   inter-   extra- |

1. _____enter

2. _____happy

3. _____ordinary

4. _____mobile

5. _____respect

6. _____national

7. _____colored

8. _____fiction

Choose four words from above. Write a sentence using each word.

9. _____

10. _____

11. _____

12. _____

Unscramble It

Unscramble the word below. Then write as many words as you can using the letters in the word.

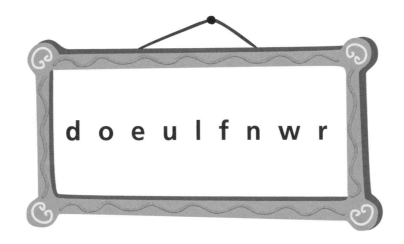

d o e u l f n w r

_____   _____

_____   _____

_____   _____

_____   _____

_____   _____

Seeing the Light

Will light pass through or bounce off each item? Write **pass through** or **bounce off** next to each picture.

1. _____

2. _____

3. _____

4. _____

5. _____

6. _____

Digging Up the Past

Jorge is an archaeologist. He finds things that people used long ago. Circle the things that Jorge is likely to find at an ancient Native American site.

Out of Sight!

The **gh** in the word **sight** is silent. Answer the questions about **gh**.

1. What are two words that end in the **gh** sound?

_____   _____

2. What are three words that end in **ght**?

_____   _____   _____

3. What are three words that rhyme with **sight**?

_____   _____   _____

Grocery Stories

Solve the problems.

1. Sara went shopping with her mom. They spent $15 on fruits and vegetables and $18 on meats. How much did they spend in all? _____

2. The grocery store is selling milk this week for 50 cents off. A gallon of milk is normally $3.60. How much will a gallon of milk cost this week? _____

3. A box of cereal is $3.14. A can of soup is $1.23. How much do the cereal and soup cost together? _____

4. Jeff buys a box of crackers, a jar of applesauce, and a loaf of bread. The crackers are $1.20. The applesauce is $1.30. Jeff spends $4.00. How much does the loaf of bread cost? _____

Racing Numbers!

Solve the riddles.

1. The number on Wanda's racing shirt is 12. Carolyn's racing number is 15 more than Jake's. Jake's is 3 less than Wanda's. What is the number on Carolyn's shirt?

   _____

2. The number on Cooper's racing shirt is 7. Jordan's racing number is 12 more than Tara's. Tara's number is 8 more than Cooper's. What is the number on Jordan's shirt?

   _____

3. The number on William's shirt is 3. Latoya's number is 8 less than the number on Jenna's shirt. Jenna's number is 17 more than William's. What is the number on Latoya's shirt?

   _____

4. The number on Vito's shirt is 15. Kara's number is 2 more than the number on Lori's shirt. Lori's number is 5 more than Vito's. What is the number on Kara's shirt?

   _____

Make Your Own Problems!

Write ten number sentences for each number below. Write both addition and subtraction sentences.

28

1. _____
2. _____
3. _____
4. _____
5. _____

6. _____
7. _____
8. _____
9. _____
10. _____

19

11. _____
12. _____
13. _____
14. _____
15. _____

16. _____
17. _____
18. _____
19. _____
20. _____

Healthy Food Choices

Circle the healthiest food in each group.

1. breakfast

2. lunch

3. snack

4. drink

5. dinner

6. dessert

Moon Changes

Draw the next moon shape in the patterns below.

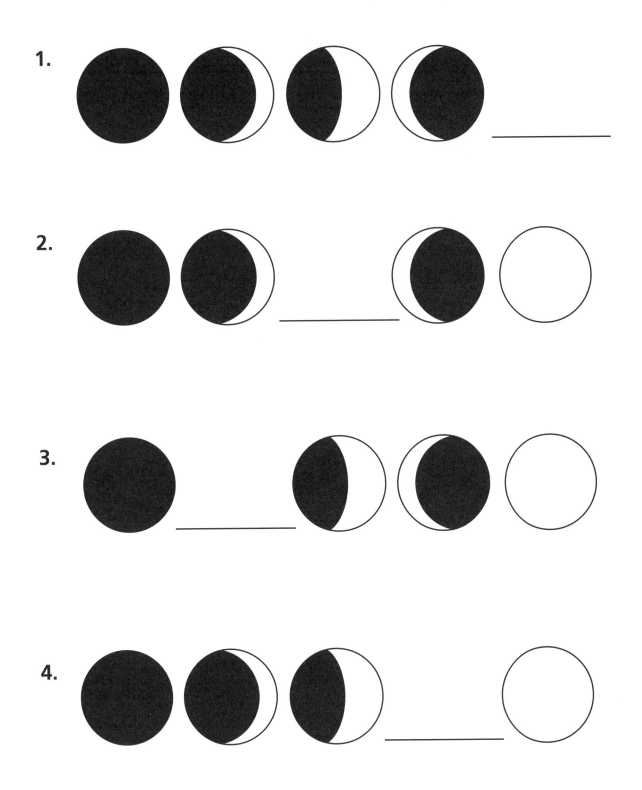

Once Upon a Time . . .

Write your own beginning to this story.

_____

_____

_____

_____

_____

_____

_____

And so the fairy was happy that the creature decided to change his terrible ways. Everyone in the forest lived happily ever after.

Elephant Matchup

Draw a line to match the addition sentence on the left to the subtraction sentence on the right that has the same answer.

12 + 3

13 + 4

15 + 4

7 + 9

10 + 10

18 + 3

12 + 2

20 − 0

23 − 7

20 − 5

22 − 3

17 − 3

19 − 2

25 − 4

It's Electric!

Look at the pictures. Circle the items that are powered by electricity.

This Week's Weather

Predict the temperature for the last day of the chart. Circle the best answer.

1.

101°	99°	98°	
Monday	Tuesday	Wednesday	Thursday

96°   69°

2.

45°	49°	52°	
Sunday	Monday	Tuesday	Wednesday

30°   50°

3.

65°	67°	68°	
Saturday	Sunday	Monday	Tuesday

72°   27°

4. Keep a record of the temperature outside for one week. Record the temperatures on the chart below.

Sunday	Monday	Tuesday	Wednesday	Thursday	Friday	Saturday

It's Time!

Read each problem.
Write the time on the clock to show the answer.

1. Jeff gets out of school at 3:00. He gets home 22 minutes later. When does Jeff get home from school?

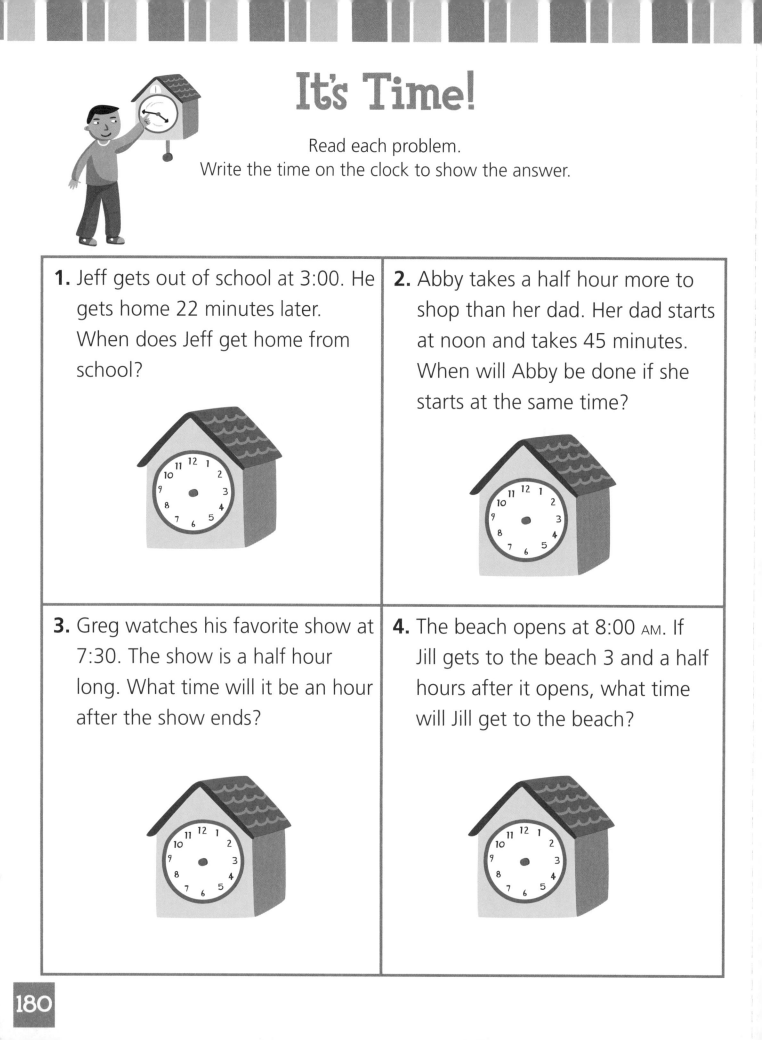

2. Abby takes a half hour more to shop than her dad. Her dad starts at noon and takes 45 minutes. When will Abby be done if she starts at the same time?

3. Greg watches his favorite show at 7:30. The show is a half hour long. What time will it be an hour after the show ends?

4. The beach opens at 8:00 AM. If Jill gets to the beach 3 and a half hours after it opens, what time will Jill get to the beach?

A Day on the Trail

The story order is mixed up. Number the paragraphs in the correct order.

_____ "We made it!" Jessie said as they saw their mom's car in the distance. "That was a fun hike. We should do it again sometime. But first, let's go swimming!" said Linda.

_____ "Bye, Mom," the girls yelled as they climbed out of the car and walked to the beginning of the forest trail. Jessie and Linda were excited to go on their first hike of the season. They would follow the red trail markers and the trail would take them to the other end of the parking lot in about a half hour. Their mom would be waiting on the other side.

_____ The girls sat down on a large rock and opened their backpacks halfway through the trail. They were both hungry and thirsty. Jessie suggested that they take a dip in the lake after they finished their hike. "Mom has our bathing suits and towels in the car with her," Jessie said.

Push or Pull?

Circle the pictures that show a push. Make a square around the pictures that show a pull.

Measuring Triangles

Add the length of each side of the triangles.

1.

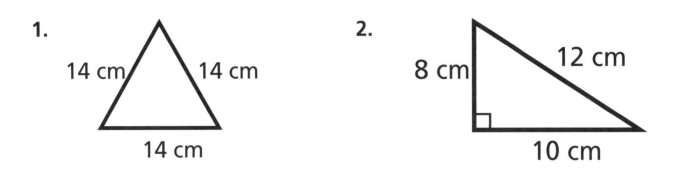

14 cm   14 cm

14 cm

_____

2.

8 cm   12 cm

10 cm

_____

3.

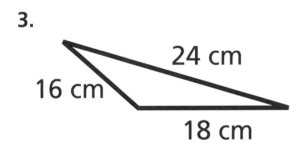

24 cm

16 cm

18 cm

_____

4.

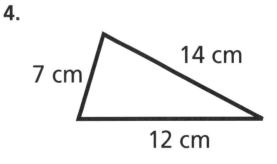

7 cm   14 cm

12 cm

_____

Match That Habitat!

Match each animal to the place where it lives.

A Buggy Riddle

Use the key below to solve the riddle. Each letter matches up with a number.
Write the letters that make up the answers to the addition problems.

A	B	C	D	E	F	G	H	I	J	K	L	M
20	11	14	7	27	6	2	21	31	10	16	9	12

N	O	P	Q	R	S	T	U	V	W	X	Y	Z
25	29	15	5	24	34	19	23	3	22	8	13	33

What do you call an ant in space?

10 + 10   11 + 14

____   ____

12 + 8   17 + 8   13 + 6   12 + 12   15 + 14   14 + 11   11 + 9   17 + 6   14 + 5

____   ____   ____   ____   ____   ____   ____   ____   ____!

Answer Key

Page 4

Page 5
1. fl
2. ch
3. pl
4. ch
5. sc
6. fl
7. sl
8. ph

Page 6
Answers will vary.

Page 7

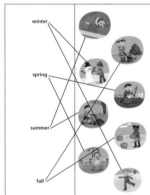

Page 8

Page 9
1. sk
2. ch
3. ng
4. ck
5. th
6. mp
7. lf
8. rm

Page 10
The following should be circled: plastic cup, rubber ducky, and small beach ball

Page 11
1. 18
2. 25
3. 50
4. 55; 75

Page 12
1. <
2. <
3. >
4. >
5. <
6. >
7. <
8. <
9. >
10. <

Page 13
1. doctor
2. waiter
3. zookeeper
4. pilot
5. chef
6. mail carrier
7. firefighter
8. construction worker
9. musician
10. photographer

Page 14

Page 15
1. A ladybug looks for food inside a house but accidentally gets lost.
2. a house
3. The ladybug decides to live in the house for the winter.

Page 16
1. crocodile
2. lizard
3. snake
4. turtle
5. chameleon
6. alligator

Page 17
1. 453, 738, 812
2. 329, 604, 818
3. 200, 213, 892
4. 122, 210, 323
5. 514, 528, 568

6. 468, 669, 839

Page 18
1. 160, 221, 700, 800
2. 911, 918, 929, 932
3. 272, 306, 421, 713
4. 202, 436, 611, 882
5. 102, 370, 709, 902

Page 19
1. rose
2. apple
3. bone
4. jar
5. lamb
6. should

Page 20
1. New Year's Eve
2. Halloween
3. 4th of July
4. Valentine's Day
5. Thanksgiving
6. Earth Day

Page 21
Needs may include food, drinks, clothing, and shelter. The list of wants may vary.

Page 22
1. cracker
2. onion
3. cherry
4. French fries
List may vary.

Page 23
1. made; ate; raced
2. reading; closed; wrote
3. cooked; cleared; washed
4. look; lost; search
5. saw; burying; barking; digging
6. brushed; took; put

Page 24

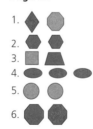

Page 25
1. true
2. false
3. false
4. true
5. true

Page 26
Answers will vary depending on personal information.

Page 27
1. bald eagle
2. White House
3. Statue of Liberty
4. flag

Possible response: Freedom means being able to do things you want.

Page 28
1. taste; smell
2. smell; touch
3. sound; sight
4. touch; sight
5. touch; smell

Page 29

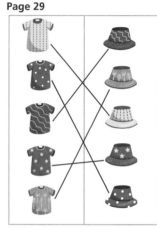

Page 30

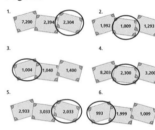

Page 31
1. a
2. c
3. b

Page 32

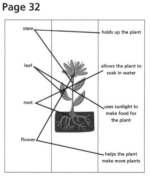

Page 33
1. now; then
2. then; now
3. now; then
4. then; now
5. now; then
6. now; then

Page 34
1. 4,290; 7,039; 9,099
2. 1,008; 2,083; 5,257
3. 8,220; 8,320; 8,620
4. 3,115; 3,151; 3,273
5. 2,273; 4,982; 8,893
6. 5,918; 5,981; 6,123

Page 35
1. greatest
2. store
3. party
4. wonderful
5. scared
6. stuck
7. soon
8. stay
9. interesting
10. eat

Page 36
1. He felt sad because his beach birthday party was cancelled due to rain.
2. His parents had planned a surprise birthday party indoors.
3. His dad, mom, and all of his party guests.

Page 37
The following items should be checked: body, front fork, foot peg, tail pipe

Page 38

1.
2.
3.
4.
5.
6.

Page 39
1. 12; 11
2. 20; 20
3. 15; 21
4. 400; 300
5. 28; 32
6. 50; 60

Page 40
1. 1610
2. from the Roman god with the same name
3. Answers will vary.

Page 41
Only rhyming words are possible answers.
1. chair; care, scare, hair
2. shoe; blue, moo, grew
3. lamp; camp, stamp, tramp
4. phone; grown, shone, flown
5. egg; beg, peg, leg
6. car; star, far, tar
7. pen; hen, ten, again
8. kite; fight, bight, tight

Page 42
1. red, blue, yellow
2. purple
3. green
4. orange

Page 43
Possible answers:

Page 44 (column 2)
1. smooth; hard
2. soft; furry
3. cold; slippery
4. soft; mushy
5. thin; bumpy
6. hard; bumpy

Page 44
Possible answers:
1. helps people to learn
2. works in a library and lends books to people
3. rules, or governs, a town
4. sells goods to people

Page 45
1. 9
2. 3
3. 3
4. 0
5. 5
6. tens
7. hundreds
8. tens
9. ones
10. ones

Page 46
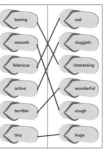

Page 47
1. dogs
2. foxes
3. wolves
4. deer
5. sheep
6. geese
7. giraffes
8. rabbits
9. butterflies
10. ponies

Page 48
1. Possible answers: magazines, books, newspapers, television, Internet, photo albums
2. 1825
3. digital

Page 49
Pictures will vary to show family events and celebrations.

Page 50

Page 51
1. loud
2. soft
3. high
4. low
Possible answers:
5. bird chirp, flute
6. truck starting; concert

Page 52

Drawings should show an invention that shows how writing will change in the future.

Page 53
Check that children use appropriate adjectives to describe each item according to their personal experiences.

Page 54
1. between New Jersey and New York City
2. 12 million
3. on the Wall of Names
4. the Statue of Liberty

Page 55

Page 56
1. $10
2. $20
3. $5
4. $200
5. $15
6. $2.50
7. $15
8. $100
9. $20
10. $1.50

Page 57

1.
2.
3.
4.
5.

Page 58
1. There is one star for each of the 50 states.
2. There is one stripe for each of the 13 original colonies.
3. Stars and Stripes, and Old Glory
4. Drawings will vary.

Page 59
My favorite thing to do is read. I love to read on the beach. I read in my tree house in my yard. And I read before I go to bed at night. I love when I finish one book and can then start reading about another new adventure. I have read about pirates and fairies. I have read long books and short books. Reading is great!

Page 60
Possible answers:
Goods: food, drinks, stuffed animals, T-shirts, souvenirs
Services: shows, amusement rides, waiter services, pictures

Page 61
4, 7, 6, 5, 2, 3, 1

Page 62
1. beef, chicken fish, eggs, nuts, beans
2. muscles, hair, organs, nails
3. stomach

Page 63
Sammy the squirrel forgot where he hid his pile of nuts for winter. His friend Leo helped him collect a new pile, and then Sammy found the ones he lost. They shared the extra nuts and had a good winter.

Page 64
1. 6:15
2. 4:45
3. 8:35
4. 2:15
5. 8:30
6. 12:45

Page 65
1. May
2. October
3. March
4. February
5. January
6. August

Page 66
1. North America
2. South America
3. Australia
4. North America
5. Europe
6. Antarctica

Page 67
1. It can save the lives of your family members in the case of a fire.
2. Answers will vary.

Page 68
1. 8
2. 24
3. 9
4. 30
5. $4.25
6. 9

Page 69
1. solid; gas
2. solid; gas
3. solid; liquid
4. solid; liquid

Page 70
1. west
2. right
3. west
4. east
5. south; west

Page 71
1. great*est*
2. tast*ier*
3. sweet*est*
4. fast*er*
5. funn*ier*
6. happi*est*

Page 72
Story endings will vary.

Page 73
1. 4 inches
2. 3 inches
3. ½ inch
4. 1 inch
5. 5 inches
6. 2 inches

Page 74
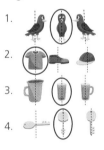

Page 75
1. 10
2. 12
3. 15
4. 48

Page 76

Page 77
Story middles will vary.

Page 78

Page 79
1. south
2. south
3. left

Page 80
1. 6
2. 8
3. 2
4. 5
5. 5
6. 10
7. 6
8. 6

Page 81
1. 7:15
2. 9:30
3. 10:45
4. 2:40
5. 6:10
6. 4:20

Page 82
1. She is happy that dinner is ready so that she does not have to watch Maya anymore.
2. Endings will vary.

Page 83

1. 2:15   **2.** 12:30
3. 8:45   **4.** 7:20
5. 3:10   **6.** 6:50

Page 84
1. 3:15
2. 5:45
3. 6:20
4. 7:40
5. 12:15
6. 1:30

Page 85
1. Carlos
2. Carlos's mom and dad
3. terrible, awful
4. cheerful, helpful, gladly

Page 86
Possible answers:

I need **air** because **I must breathe to stay alive.** I also need **food** because **my body needs energy to stay alive.** And I also need **water** because **my body is made mostly of water.**

Page 87
Stories will vary but should use descriptive words.

Page 88
I went to my favorite library with my mom today. We got out of the car in the parking lot. We went east to get into the library. After I looked for books, we walked south to get to the playground. After I played for a while, we walked west to look in the greenhouse. Then we went north to get back to our car and go home.

Page 89
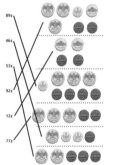

Pages 90–91
Play should use exact dialogue from page 90.

Page 92
1. 8 years
2. 1801
3. 1817
4. John Adams
5. 4
6. 1825

Page 93
8 Over the Clouds
6 My Favorite Foods
5 Monsters Eat Garbage
3 Call Me Your Friend
9 Silly Puppies
1 Antarctica
2 Apples, Pears, and Bananas
7 Oh My Goodness!
4 Captain Tube Socks
10 Stories of the Second Grade

Page 94
1. 75°
2. 40°
3. 32°
4. 105°
5. 81°
6. 63°

Page 95
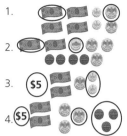

Page 96

Page 97
1. one mile
2. six million years
3. 277 miles
4. rushing water from the Colorado River
5. amazing views, interesting wildlife

Page 98
Vacation
Possible words:
cat
ton
tin
not
tan
can

Page 99
Stories will vary.

Page 100
1. 152
2. 421
3. 775
4. 222

Page 101
1. Florida
2. Hawaii
3. Alaska
4. Michigan
5. Texas
6. Kansas
7. Washington
8. Rhode Island

Page 102

Page 103
1. mountain
2. canyon, valley
3. plain
4. canyon, mountain
5. plain
6. Possible answers: high, rocky, rugged
7. Possible answers: flat, grassy, wide

Page 104
Possible answers:
1. I can reduce my use of paper by writing on both sides of it.
2. I can reuse plastic jars by cleaning them and storing toys in them.
3. I can recycle newspapers by collecting them and putting them out with the recycling.

Page 105
1. opinion
2. fact
3. opinion
4. fact
5. opinion
6. fact

Page 106
1. notebook
2. book
3. toy car
4. telephone
5. crayons
6. ball

Page 107
1. cylinder
2. triangular prism
3. cube
4. pyramid
5. cone
6. hexagonal prism

Page 108
1. It lives in water, so it must breathe with gills.
2. Its legs get longer
3. It lives on land, so it must breathe with lungs.
4. Possible answer: butterfly

Page 109
1. false
2. true
3. true
4. false
5. false

Page 110
1. 15 minutes
2. 20 minutes
3. 10 minutes
4. 2:00

Page 111
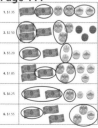

Page 112

Page 113
Drawings will vary.

Page 114
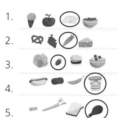
1.
2.
3.
4.
5.

Page 115
following information:
Summer: warm weather, more hours of daylight, large green leaves
Winter: cold weather, fewer hours of daylight, no leaves
Both: outdoor fun

Page 116
1. Ricky Barber
Becca Bear
Sue Black
Janice Brown

2. Zachary Zap
Carrie Zebra
Marcus Zipper
Michael Zucchini

3. Jake Handshake
Hanki Hippo
Harry Hockey
Carol Humor

4. Larry Saturn
Jessica Sleepy
Susie Social
George Street

Page 117
Check that children have drawn each shape.
1. sphere
2. cube
3. pyramid
4. rectangular prism

Page 118
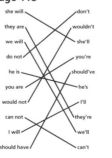

she will — don't
they are — wouldn't
we will — she'll
do not — you're
he is — should've
you are — he's
would not — I'll
can not — they're
I will — we'll
should have — can't

Page 119
1. She did not want to ruin the surprise of what Sophie's gift was.
2. Yes, because she bought the clothes for the doll, so she probably bought the doll also.
3. Predictions will vary.

Page 120
1. thermometer
2. balance
3. ruler
4. measuring cup
5. thermometer
6. ruler

Page 121
1. 14
2. 6
3. 3
4. 12

Page 122
1. 3; 10; 3/10
2. 2; 8; 2/8
3. 5; 12; 5/12
4. 6; 14; 6/14
5. 1; 6; 1/6
6. 4; 10; 4/10

Page 123
1. plane
2. truck
3. ship
4. truck

Page 124
Letters will vary, but should include a description of a problem and a possible solution.

Page 125
1. $2.45
2. $1.35
3. $5.53
4. $3.30
5. $3.15
6. $1.28

Page 126
1. 427
2. 29
3. 842
4. 8,000

Page 127

Page 128
1. self*fish*
2. understand*able*
3. reck*less*
4. paint*er*
5. real*ize*
6. sudden*ly*
7. excite*ment*
8-10. Check that sentences correctly use one of the words in 1-7.

Page 129
Adjectives will vary.

Page 130
1. during the Civil War
2. Angel of the Battlefield
3. The American Red Cross
4. helps victims of disasters

Page 131
1. 27
2. 18
3. 50
4. 8

Page 132

Page 133
1. ounces
2. pounds
3. ounces
4. pounds
5. ounces
6. ounces

Page 134
1. I can't wait for summer to be here.
2. My dog will be so happy to see me every day.
3. Mom says I can go to the beach and to the pool.
4. I hope I can invite some friends to come with me.
5. We will stay out and play until the sun goes down.
6. Then we will play again the next day, too.

Page 135

Paper	Plastic	Metal
newspapers	juice jug	can of beans
magazines	soda bottle	coffee can
milk container	bird seed jug	
cereal box		

Page 136
Check that children draw the appropriate foods in each part of the pyramid.

Page 137
1. in the future
2. the characters use gadgets that do not yet exist
3. in Leo's kitchen
4. Leo and his mom

Page 138
1. 1
2. 4
3. 6
4. 4

Page 139

1.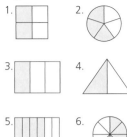

Page 140
1. country
2. city
3. city; country
4. country
5. city
6. country
Answers will vary

Page 141
Story endings will vary.

Page 142

Page 143
1. Wash Your Face
3 Add soap and lather it on your face.
2 Fix the temperature of the water.
5 Dry your face with a towel.
4 Rinse the soap from your face.
1 Turn on the water at the sink.
2. Write a Book Report
4 Write about what you thought of the book.
1 Choose the book you want to read.
5 Read what you wrote to fix mistakes.
2 Read the book.
3 Think about what the book was about.
3. Check your e-mail
4 Click on e-mails marked "NEW."
3 Open your e-mail program.
2 Log in your password.
5 Write a response to your e-mails.
1 Turn on your computer.

Page 144
Be sure that children color in a fraction of each shape and then write the corresponding fraction in numbers.

Page 145
1. 3
2. 4
3. leapfrog
4. jacks

Page 146
Because it is two tired!

Page 147

Page 148
Possible answers:
1. so a car does not hit you
2. so you do not hurt other people
3. so you stay safer in an accident
4. so the driver can easily see you
5. to protect your head from injury

Page 149
1. 2/8
2. 4/5
3. 1/3
4. ¼

Page 150
1. May
2. 20
3. 20
4. 30

Page 151
1. 25
2. 12
3. 3
4. 7
5. 13

Page 152
1. She feels sad to not be included in the group of girls.
2. She feels happy to be included in the group of girls.
3. Possible answer: The girls may have noticed that Abby was alone and decided to include her.
4. Predictions will vary.

Page 153
Possible answers:
1. fun
2. tasty
3. tired
4. scared
5. serious
6. short
7. unfinished
8. delicious
9. unhappily
10. happy

Page 154
She wanted to catch a wave.

Page 155

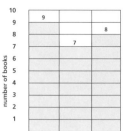

Page 156
1. 27
2. 11
3. 28
4. 29
5. 3
6. 7
7. 30
8. 27
9. 4

Page 157
Stories and drawings will vary.

Page 158
1. b
2. a
3. b

Page 159

Page 160

Page 161
1. 7
2. 11
3. 19
4. 9

Page 162
Letters will vary but should include what the child is doing over summer vacation.

Page 163

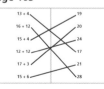

Page 164
1. 6
2. 2
3. 5
4. 10
5. 2
6. 6
7. 6
8. 12
9. 23
10. 27

Page 165

Page 166
1. reenter
2. unhappy
3. extraordinary
4. automobile
5. disrespect
6. international
7. multicolored
8. nonfiction
9–12. Check that sentences correctly use one of the words in 1–8.

Page 167
Wonderful
Possible words:
won
wonder
done
fuel
fold
row
run
fun
wed
flow
flew
low
frown
flown

Page 168
1. pass through
2. bounce off
3. bounce off
4. bounce off
5. pass through
6. pass through

Page 169

Page 170
Possible answers:
1. sigh, high
2. height, might, flight, light
3. tight, bite, kite, right, night

Page 171
1. $33
2. $3.10
3. $4.37
4. $1.50

Page 172
1. 24
2. 27
3. 12
4. 22

Page 173
Possible number sentences:

1.	28 + 0	6.	28 – 0
2.	27 + 1	7.	30 – 2
3.	25 + 3	8.	35 – 7
4.	12 + 16	9.	37 – 9
5.	18 + 10	10.	40 – 12

11.	18 + 1	16.	21 – 2
12.	15 + 4	17.	25 – 6
13.	13 + 6	18.	27 – 8
14.	10 + 9	19.	24 – 5
15.	7 + 12	20.	30 – 11

Page 174

1. breakfast
2. lunch
3. snack
4. drink
5. dinner
6. dessert

Page 175
1. full moon
2. quarter moon
3. waxing crescent
4. waning gibbous

Page 176
Story beginnings will vary.

Page 177
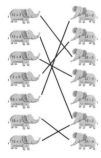

Page 178

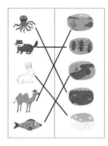

Page 179
1. 96°
2. 50°
3. 72°
4. Child's chart should record temperatures at approximately the same time each day.

Page 180
1.
2.
3.
4.

Page 181
3 "We made it!" Jessie said as they saw their mom's car in the distance. "That was a fun hike. We should do it again sometime. But first, let's go swimming!" said Linda.

1 "Bye, Mom," the girls yelled as they climbed out of the car and walked to the beginning of the forest trail. Jessie and Linda were excited to go on their first hike of the season. They would follow the red trail markers and the trail would take them to the other end of the parking lot in about a half hour. Their mom would be waiting on the other side.

2 The girls sat down on a large rock and opened their backpacks halfway through the trail. They were both hungry and thirsty. Jessie suggested that they take a dip in the lake after they finished their hike. "Mom has our bathing suits and towels in the car with her," Jessie said.

Page 182

Page 183
1. 42 cm
2. 30 cm
3. 58 cm
4. 33 cm

Page 184

Page 185
An antronaut!